Margo
Queen of Country & Irish

MARGO WAS GIRL SINGER OF THE YEAR

FOR 1970

SPOTLIGHT MAGAZINE POLL

This book is the life story of one of Ireland's best-loved Country singers, Margo. It celebrates her fifty years in the music world. Born in Donegal, she went on to become known all over Ireland and abroad, especially within the emigrant communities of England and America.

Margo

Queen of Country & Irish

The Promise and the Dream

MARGARET O'DONNELL

THE O'BRIEN PRESS
DUBLIN

First published 2014 by
The O'Brien Press Ltd,
12 Terenure Road East, Rathgar,
Dublin 6, Ireland.
Tel: +353 1 4923333; Fax: +353 1 4922777
E-mail: books@obrien.ie
Website: www.obrien.ie
Reprinted 2014.

ISBN: 978-1-84717-674-5

3 5 7 8 6 4 2
14 16 18 19 17 15

Printed and bound by ScandBook AB, Sweden
The paper in this book is produced using pulp from managed forests

Acknowledgements

To all my friends, thank you, you all know how special you are to me. To everyone I mentioned in the book, thank you for being part of my life.

One person who is important in my life is Clive who takes care of my music and my shows. Clive came into my life close to twenty years ago and he is caring and understanding towards me at all times. We can meet each other and we seem to pick up where we left off as if we've never been apart. Clive is a wonderful musician and I appreciate his friendship. I feel I don't have to explain our friendship and to tell you the truth I don't think I could if I tried. All I want to say is 'Thank you, Clive, you are special to me.

I want to thank everyone I had the pleasure of meeting through my sing-ing. Most importantly of all are the fans and the strangers who have become my friends. Thank you to all the DJs at home and elsewhere who play my music and to the journalists who keep my name out there in the public eye.

A lot of journalists have written articles about Margo over the years, but the first person ever to write about me was my dear friend and native Don-egal man, Donal K O'Boyle. Through all my ups and downs, Donal never wrote one negative word about me. He still writes to this day and is one of my closest friends. I will never forget these great people and Donal is defi-nitely one of them.

I write songs with Joe McShane, a special man from County Armagh, who now lives in Chicago. He is very dear to me and is also a wonderful talent.

A special word for the people who helped me in any way while I was writing my book, all of it written in longhand. I don't own a computer and can't type, so thanks, Bridie and Shirley. I mention many people in this book without giving all the names. The reason I was hesitant initially about writing my story was that I felt I would have to name everyone. But recently I went on holiday and one evening as I sat by the pool, a man called Shaun handed me a book to read. It was *My House of Memories* by Country legend Merle Haggard. As I read it I realised he had said everything he wanted to say but without actually naming people. I told Shaun that he had solved a problem for me and I could now see how to write my own story. I said I'd tell my readers that it was he who had shown me the way. He said, 'Would you, really?' All I will say is Shaun is a singer and a very nice guy. Thank you, Shaun. I keep my promises!

Margo

Contents

PROLOGUE

People have asked me many, many times if I would ever write the story of my life and my answer has always been the same: maybe someday. I do believe there is a book in every single person but not everyone chooses to tell their life story to the world. That was my feeling too. My journey through life is mine and no-one knows how to live that journey but me. However, I am now approaching fifty golden years in the music business and because of that I feel a little inspired to share some of my private and public moments, high times and low times, good times and bad.

My story will be difficult for me to tell. I have to write it the way it happened. And that means it will be like confessing and also facing some sad, bad and unhappy times in my life. My feeling is that it has to be the truth, otherwise it would be worthless. I have been told over the years by various people that my story has helped them in different ways and if this book helps just one other person along the way then I will be glad I put pen to paper.

Being a successful singer and so much in the public eye means, of course, that my private life is so much more on display and a matter for discussion than if I were the ordinary girl from Kincasslagh who had never gone on stage. But that is part of the show-business life. However, that's not to say that I am immune to rumour and gossip. Many parts of my private life have been up for discussion over the years, sometimes giving rise to ridiculous claims about me. At the end of the day, no one really knows me but me. Unless, as the saying goes, 'you have walked in my shoes' you can't know the true me. I feel the time has come to set the record straight.

It has not all been about smelling the roses, and there are parts of my life that I have hesitated to talk about, but in order to let you into my life as I have lived it, I must tell it. Many times I stumbled but I managed to get back up on my feet again and continue on life's journey. During those dark days I would always see a faint flicker of light that made me reach out and go forward; my will to succeed was always greater than any failure.

I have been blessed that my singing career has taken me to so many places; each has special memories for me that time can never erase. I have sung on many huge stages with so many legends of Country music and I feel I have achieved all the accolades there are and I have done all that I wanted to do. Of course I have regrets, too – a major one is not having children – although some rumours over the years say different! I wish those rumours were true.

Will I stop singing? Not as long as people want me to sing. Although health issues prevent me from touring the way I used to, I am still performing and still meeting all those wonderful people who have been so loyal to me throughout the years. Every day I thank God for the special gift I was given and what it has enabled me to achieve. As I look back over my life and all the events that were part of it I seem to have been learning all along the way. Learning from the experiences, both good and bad, that have shaped who I am today. Even now, when there is such contentment in my life, I still feel there is a lot to learn.

Because I started singing at such a young age – I was only thirteen when I joined the Keynotes – I suppose it was inevitable that my naiveté and inexperience would be exploited. Many times I trusted people and many times I have been disappointed. Many times I have helped others who then turn around and mistreated me later. I have been hurt by some close to me who should have been most concerned for my welfare.

Life has come full circle for me. Donegal will always be where I am from and no-one will ever know how proud I am of that, but that part of my life is gone. I will always be proud of my heritage. Now my home is where I am happiest and 'where I hang my hat'. I have a few close friends whom I treasure and the wonderful fans who still come to see me and who are part of my extended family.

I am very aware of what I have written in this book and I want people to know that no matter what has happened to me in my life I do not feel bitterness towards anyone or anything – but I had to deal with extreme hurt and I will always have this hurt in the back of my mind. My counsellor always advised me to get rid of anger but not to forget, that way I will not go down the road of hurt again. My first No 1 record was suitably called 'I'll Forgive and I'll Try to Forget'; there's just one word there that doesn't fit;

the word is 'try', because I can never. But I have never felt jealous of anyone, hence I have true contentment within.

Writing this book has brought both joy and sorrow as I relive the experiences of a full life, both in and out of the spotlight. I hope that all of you who read it will feel that you know a little bit more about Margo/Margaret O'Donnell. I thank you for always being there. I became Margo after I joined the Keynotes. We were booked to play in the Mulroy Ballroom in Kerrykeel, County Donegal. The hall was owned by John Kerr, a balladeer, and when we arrived, we saw a poster with the words: 'Appearing tonight, Margo and The Keynotes' – and that's how Margaret O'Donnell became Margo!

The title of my book: *The Promise and the Dream*, is based on a pledge I made to my father on the day of his death, a promise I took so seriously it almost destroyed me – not the promise itself but the way in which I handled it. I felt I had to honour it, but I went beyond what was expected of me. 'The Dream' in the title refers to a dream I had for me and my family: that we would achieve security, happiness and success in our lives and that I would do all in my power to realise that dream for them all. Sometimes what we want and dream about does not work out as we would like it to, but it is all part of God's plan. The great things I achieved were what was intended in my life. I feel we are only given what we can handle and someone else takes over and brings it further. The dream started with me, Margo, and was definitely brought to another level by my brother Daniel, so you see both the promise and the dream have been fulfilled.

A Special Note: My Mother

My, how time can change the story of one's life. Time has changed the story of my autobiography too. I completed it last year and it is now coming close to publication in autumn 2014. I have to bring my life story up to date. We lost two special people this year. Mam's brother, Owen McGonagle, who lived in Carlisle, in England, passed away on 15 January; he was the youngest of the McGonagle siblings. Then Mam herself, who would have celebrated her ninety-fifth birthday in July, was called home by God on 18 May. I was looking forward so much to giving my mam the first signed copy of my book, but now that cannot be. However, I am so happy that before she passed away I read for her every word I wrote in the book. I wanted her blessing on it all and I got that from her, and for that I'm grateful.

Mam and I came through many happy and sad times together. After Dad passed away things and times were tough, but we rallied together and we made it through. Our first-ever home was a beautiful council cottage which we moved into in 1967 and we were all so happy; then tragedy had struck on 16 August 1968 when we lost Dad, but in the early seventies I was able to buy the cottage outright for my mam and that made her feel secure. I was able to help Mam financially through the years and we never went without. And even though Dad had passed away, I felt he was always watching over us.

My mother was a strong person and I was always amazed at

how she could adapt to the changes life brought. Mam loved the spotlight and loved all the fame life bestowed on her. She could chat to both Daniel's and my fans as if they were her friends too, but she was equally proud of her children John Bosco, James and Kathleen. As the years went by, Mam confided in me about everything and we grew closer. Before she died I spoke to her about going to Dad and God in Heaven. I also told her she was all I had as I didn't have a partner, but that I didn't want her to be afraid of dying. When she passed I lost a very dear friend and it broke my heart to lose her. But to my mam I gave my all and, thankfully, I don't have any regrets. May she rest in peace.

FROM MY MOTHER:

I am really happy that Margaret has written her book and I know everyone who reads it will enjoy it. Since Margaret started with the Keynotes back in 1964 she has not had it easy and life has been very difficult for her. Margaret has always helped me, especially when her Dad died in 1968 and has always been there for me when I needed her. I am so proud of Margaret and I want to thank her for all she has been to me down through the years. Margaret has read her book for me and I know everyone will enjoy it just as much as I have.

Love you always,

Mammy

To My Mother

As I sat and watched your last few days
Many memories I recalled
My tears of loss and special thoughts
Of times long past and gone

The legacy you left behind is there for all to see
But most of all, dear Mother, I thought of you and me
Times we had together and many hills we climbed
Somehow we managed every one
Taking one step at a time

I hope I made you happy and didn't cause you too much pain
Then I can say with hand on heart my love for you was not in vain

I know you are with Dad right now and God is close to you
So watch over me and keep me safe in all I have to do
I love you both with all my heart and I'll always hold you near
Though when I recall the times we shared I know I'll shed a tear

Give a kiss to Dad for me, tell him I love him so
Dear Mam, I'll always love you more than you could ever know
Rest with God, dear parents, you deserve to be together
The love you share no one can touch and it will last for ever.

Chapter 1

My Humble Beginnings

My childhood memories are really precious. Today I listen to stories of the miserable childhoods of some children and I realise how blessed I was and the simple things that made my life complete. We were so happy and carefree. I had my family, neighbours and close friends around me. I was safe at all times. I was important to all I came in contact with. Most of the friendships I formed then have lasted a lifetime. There were no sleepless nights or bad dreams. I would play hard all day like all children and lie in bed at night in a peaceful sleep. I had no fear of anything in my life and I felt so privileged to have so much love around me.

My story began in Donegal Town Community Hospital on 6 February 1951 and, apparently, even in those early days I had a great set of lungs! I was named Margaret Catherine O'Donnell, after both grandmothers, Margaret on my mother's side and Catherine on my father's. I have been told that I was poorly as a new baby and had to be christened in the hospital rather than going to a church for the ceremony. For the same reason my godparents were not family or close friends. My godfather was a man from Glencolmcille by the name of Breslin, who was visiting his wife in the hospital. I recently spoke to one of his daughters, Kathleen Meehan, and she shared some lovely stories about him. My godmother was sixteen-year-old Mary McDaid, who was a patient in the hospital getting her appendix out and had befriended my mother. Mary moved to England in later life and many years later I was singing with the Keynotes in the Buffalo Ballroom in Camden Town in London, when after the dance a man came up to speak to me. He told me his sister was godmother to a Margaret O'Donnell from my area and asked me if I knew her. I realised I *was* that girl; how strange life is! Through her brother I made contact with Mary and we remained close until her death some years ago. She always called me 'Maggie Moe'.

When I left hospital I was brought back to Acres in Burtonport – my father's home place. We lived with his mother for the first six months of my life before heading, like so many people from our area, to Scotland. When I was about three years of age we moved from Scotland back to Acres once again. It's funny the little things you remember as you look back on your life. I have a vague memory from those days of going to Mass with my mam, and a man by the name of Jimmy O'Donnell being very kind and giving me a threepenny bit every time he saw me outside the chapel.

After a short time living in Acres we were on the move again, this time to my mother's Uncle Ned's house in Kincasslagh, where we lived until 1967. I have wonderful memories of this house. It was a two-storey building but we only used the downstairs as I think at that time upstairs was not habitable. It had a beautiful, big, open fire with an old crane and crook and the kettle hanging from it. There was no bathroom, just a dry toilet down across the road in the little garden, but that was not uncommon for the time. The house was a real home with a warm personality. The memories, oh the memories are just wonderful. Even back then there were always visitors – a lot of fishermen from the islands would come and stay as they were often stranded on the mainland and wouldn't be able to get back to their homes. Maybe because my mother was an island woman, they knew that there would always be a bed for them in our home. Of course, when the fishermen were staying it was bad news for my brother John (also called John Bosco) and myself as we would have to sleep on the floor on a mattress.

All the people I came in contact with as a young girl were good, honest, hardworking folk; everyone helped each other, no matter what. Maybe people who owned their own business had a little more than others, but on the whole we were all the same. I really don't remember anyone being jealous of anyone else and no one ever went without. Fun in those days was simple, but then life itself was simple back then. There wasn't a car at every door, there were no computers or even a telephone, no modern-day gadgets like we have today. In our little village the public phone was in a corner of the post office. If you needed to place a call to, say, Scotland, you had to book the call in the morning for a given time in the evening.

I remember being in Dungloe on an Easter Sunday and there was a band competition; my dad played the flute at that time with the Mullaghduff Band. The pipe and flute bands marched on St Patrick's Day and the parade was held on Easter Sunday. This particular year stays in my memory more than any other. The Mullaghduff Band had just won 1st prize in the competition and I went with my dad to Cannon's Bar at the bottom of the town, where the men were having a drink to celebrate. I was about eight or nine years of age and really should not have been in the bar, but I was with my father, so I guess it was okay. Someone asked Dad to sing and he sang 'A Mother's Last Goodbye'. When he had finished they wanted more, but he declined and lifted me up on a high bar stool and said, 'This is my wee girl, Margaret, she will sing for you.' Well, I felt ten feet tall. I started singing, and the more I sang the more they clapped. A friend of my dad's, Barney Doherty, took somebody's cap and passed it around and everyone put money into it for me. When Dad and I headed for home we counted the money and we had nineteen shillings and eight pence. I looked up at my dad and he smiled and said, 'Mam will be proud of you.' I knew we could get into trouble for being late but we knew the money would get us off the hook!

Even as a child I was always very easily offended. If Mam and I had words over something – now, I am talking of when I was aged four to six – if we fell out, I would head for my bedroom, get a little brown cardboard case I had, and throw a pair of knickers, socks, vest and a nightdress into it. Then I'd put on my coat and announce that I was leaving home. Off I would go over behind the hill, where I'd sit, hoping and waiting for her to need me and come and get me. One evening, our neighbour Biddy Tague saw me and she said, 'Oh dear, have you left home again, Margaret?' I would wait but Mam would not come. I didn't know it, but she was keeping a quiet eye on me. When darkness fell I'd have to swallow my pride, and, with case in hand, frozen and hungry, I'd return home until we fell out again.

I guess the only thing that shadowed the happiness of our home in Kincasslagh during those years was my dad having to go away to work. It was always sad when he had to go. There was very little work in our area unless you were fishing on a boat and Dad was no fisherman, although he did work a couple of winters curing the fish. Sadly, most of the time it was to Scotland he had to go for work. He would come home a few times in the year, mainly at Christmas and, of course, in the summer, though not for a holiday but to cut the turf and to set the potatoes and vegetables for us.

I remember my Aunty Nappy (her real name was Bella) and her husband Jim Ward, they would come from Edinburgh each year with their families, and one year it was decided that my eldest brother John would go back with them to Edinburgh for a holiday. The day before John was to leave, Jim said to me, 'Would you like to come too?' And I did. It was a great adventure and, better still, I was going to get to see my dad. He didn't know that I was coming; he thought it was just John. I remember my aunt keeping me in the room when he arrived at their house. He was fussing around John and as he opened the kitchen door I walked in. I remember him saying to my Uncle Jim, 'You shouldn't do that, you'll give a man a heart attack.'

When I look back on my dad's absences when I was a child I can see that at the time I didn't understand it fully. I thought he was living just like us but in a different country. I didn't realise until I got older and heard stories of the hardship he endured with his brothers, what sacrifices he made for each and every one of his family. He lived with my uncles in an old, damp caravan on the site of wherever they were working. There was no hot water, no warm fire to come home to at night, no cooked dinner awaiting him after a hard day's work. The only comfort my father had was at the weekends when he would go to his brothers or sisters in Edinburgh and later to see my granny who lived in her later years with my Aunty Nappy. I remember my grandmother well. Everyone called her Gaga – today we hear of the singer Lady Gaga, but my grandmother was famous long before her! I loved Gaga, and, sadly, she lived longer than my dad. I know her heart was broken when she lost her youngest son. The sadness of losing one of your own children at such a young age must be unbearable.

My father was a talented, loyal and steadfast man. Every two weeks a registered letter would come from Scotland to my mother with money in it. I still have those letters and I often read them. He would give my mother and ourselves all the news, any advice we needed, and an explanation if the money was less or more each fortnight. In the note to Mam he would write a little line with a separate kiss for John, me, Kathleen, James and Daniel, and normally include the message: 'Be good to one another and don't forget to say your prayers.'

He was a good provider and we didn't want for anything. He loved us and he loved my mother unconditionally. He was a wonderful, wonderful father.

Dad was a great storyteller, a simple man with a warm sense of humour. You can probably tell by how much I speak of my father that I was engrossed with him, so much so that I even used to watch him shave. I remember fondly one day he was shaving and I piped up and asked him, 'Dad, where did you find me?' He replied, 'Andrew Dinny [Andrew Bonner, father of Packie Bonner, Ireland and Celtic goalkeeper, who was a great mate of my father's] and myself heard there was a baby up at Trianagh strand. Me and your Mammy wanted a wee girl, so Andrew and myself headed away up and we were looking down the strand and Andrew said, "Do you see that winkle down there, Francie, I think she is under it." So I took off. I took the cap off and I started to run as there was a tinker man running from the opposite direction to try and get to you before me, but I got you before he did.' Wasn't it some story? I believed every word as if my life depended on it. As I look back on it now I had eaten plenty of winkles when I was little and should have realised from the size of them that they wouldn't hide a baby, no matter how wee, but I have always held that story close to me, even to this day.

Other memories of my early years are of the day my sister Kathleen was born in the house where we lived at that time. At that stage I thought that mothers had to go to the hospital to get a baby and, come to think of it, my mother must have worn looser clothes then because I didn't even realise she was pregnant. I guess it is fair to say that I didn't have that type of imagination in those days and you weren't ever told that you were going to have a little brother or sister.

Anyway, on the day Kathleen was to make her debut into this world, my brother John, Biddy McGonagle and her brother Neil and myself were there with my dad, who, as you know, played the flute. Dad went down to the end of the garden and cut four little sticks which we called sally rods. He carved out little note holes in them and gave them to us. We marched up and down from the house to the pier and back and forth with our 'flutes', thinking we were the bee's knees. Every time we would come back up to the house my dad would go inside and we were told to stand outside. He would soon return and we would set off for the pier again as if we were in the band. Then on this one occasion when we returned he told us to come in, and we saw this baby. I remember looking at her and my mam telling us that the baby was a girl. I recall being very proud and my brother John asking, 'Is she really ours?' I was so proud because at last I had a sister.

Another episode that involved Kathleen was when she was four or five years of age. We used to get milk from Neil Sharkey from Lower Cruit who had a house on the mountain, about thirty or forty minutes' walk from our home. Our post office sold sweets, ice cream and various other things like that. The craze at the time was for lucky bags. My brother John and Neil McGonagle had acquired a pack of five Woodbine cigarettes and we thought the little toy cigarette plastic holders that were in the lucky bags would help keep the smell of the cigarettes away. Biddy McGonagle (Neil's sister), who was also in on the act, and myself had to buy the lucky bags and we had to feel them before we bought them to make sure we got two with the cigarette holders in them. This we did, but on the morning of the adventure both John and I fell out with Kathleen and for punishment our mam made us take her along, and our plan was destroyed. The only thing we could do was make Kathleen smoke with us. We picked up our milk and headed into a wee sort of dyke near the side of the road for our adventure. We all smoked and then we made Kathleen smoke. It was hilarious – sure we were all dizzy but we thought by smoking we were like grown ups. It was mine, John's, Neil's and Biddy's secret – and now it included Kathleen. A week went by and all was well until Kathleen again fell out with John and me and said she was going to tell about the smoking. We were sitting by the fire and didn't know Mam was at the front door and she could hear everything. Mam came in and asked, 'What smoking?' Well, Kathleen confessed and John and I were left with little red marks on our bums afterwards. How innocent we all were back then.

Scotland played an important part in my early years and I just loved it; it was like a second home to me. I used to go to my Aunty Nappy in Lewis Terrace and she was such a special and warm-hearted woman. I remember how my cousins, the Wards, would lift me up and sit me on the fridge and I would sing for them. I was putting on concerts for them as soon as I was able to talk; I guess that's the reason I have a special bond with them even to this day. John would sing too and we used to do duets together when we were little.

Which brings me to the question I am most often asked: when did I first begin to sing? Well, the simple answer is that I was probably singing from when I was three or four. I don't really remember a time when I didn't sing. I remember being a small girl listening to my local choir at Mass and being amazed at the wonderful sounds and music that came from them. Molly Sharkey, the choir mistress, had heard that I could sing and she asked me to join them. I must have been the smallest singer in the choir.

I was on stage a few years later! There were no dances held in the local village halls during the period of Lent, but they were replaced by little dramas or plays. In my area there were many halls and each one put on these little plays. I used to attend them all. During one of the intervals between drama sketches there would be music and song. It was there that I sang on a stage for the first time. I can still recall it as if it was yesterday. I sang 'The Road by the River', which I later recorded and it became a big hit for me. As I finished one of the verses, a local woman, Sarah Melly, shouted up to me, 'Good on you, my girl.' I looked down and was so distracted I forgot the start of the next verse, and I just stood there. I didn't even have the sense to walk off – the local parish priest, Father Deegan, came onto the stage and carried me off. That was my first case of stage fright, and the end of my debut, so to speak.

Plays like that were an annual event and from that night onwards I became part of the furniture on the local scene, singing a song during the intervals, or, if there was anything big happening in the area, I would be asked to sing. My mother was the driving force and always encouraged me to sing.

Another place that was important to me as a young child was Owey Island where my mother was from and where we went on holidays to see my grandparents. Every house on Owey had a cow and a donkey. I remember the beautiful long hot summers and the lovely dinners, which were always around one o'clock in the day, not in the evening like nowadays. Afterwards, all of us young ones would take the cows and go out to the mountains until late evening. This was called herding, and while the cows grazed we would entertain ourselves playing games and telling stories.

My mother's brother, James, was also someone who was special in my life. He lived on Owey Island but in his later years he moved with his wife Peggy and family and lived quite near us in Kincasslagh. While my grandparents lived on Owey, Uncle James was our means of transport to and from the island and he always rode the waves and weather with a smile to make us feel safe. The excitement of going to Owey Island was something special. Owey played a huge part in my singing career. At night time there people would meet at the school and sit on the steps or the wall and my mother would say, 'Margaret, sing', and I would. I guess I was like a remote-controlled performer! I would sing every sort of Irish ballad and even folksy songs. I couldn't read yet so my mother taught me the words. She didn't sing herself although I remember her father, my grandfather, singing a song called 'Skibbereen'. Uncle Owen, one of my mother's brothers, had a lovely voice and would sing songs such as 'The Galway Shawl' and 'The Old Bog Road'. He lived in Carlisle in England with his wife, Muriel, and only died very recently, making my mother the last of that family left alive until her death in May 2014. Uncle Edward, who lived close by in Donegal, and Aunt Margaret, who emigrated to New York as a war bride, died some years ago. Owey Island is a very different place today. I visited there with my mam and uncle a few years ago. But the memories from the old days are just wonderful and will always be with me.

On my father's side of the family there was an outpouring of music and there still is to this day; all of my cousins sing. I think my love for music and my love for the old airs can be credited to my father. Dad used to teach me the airs of songs. I remember him teaching me 'False-hearted Sweetheart' over in the old house. It was a song I didn't record until around ten years ago as it was filled with too many memories of him. Even then it was very difficult for me to record and I might have given up but for the encouragement of my musical director, Clive Culbertson, who helped me to get over my nerves in the recording studio.

My father's family, the 'Doney Owens', have always been close to us and stuck up for each other all the way. My father had six brothers and two sisters; Uncle Dinnie lived near us at home, as did Uncle Josie. My uncles Hughie, James and Con lived in Scotland with their wives and families. They were all very caring towards each other and would regularly gather at Aunt Nappy's house in Lewis Terrace. The youngest of the family was Aunty Mary who lived in Edinburgh and she was quite a character. I also had an Uncle Owen who was the eldest, but he died young and I never knew him.

All of my cousins still spend special times together and, believe me, I so look forward to our gatherings. The Doney Owens, in my eyes, reign supreme. I believe it was a sight to see the six brothers march out on St Patrick's Day in the Acres Band many years ago. I can honestly say that I am proud to have all my cousins on both sides – the O'Donnells and the McGonagles – in my life.

A Belfast family, the McGarrys, used to come to Kincasslagh every summer and they became friends with my mother. On a few occasions they took John and myself back to Belfast for a holiday. Once while we were there, 'Granny' McGarry, as we fondly called her, gave me a sixpenny piece to buy sweets. I had done a few chores for my sixpence but, so as not to leave John out, she gave him a threepenny bit. He wasn't too happy that I had double what he had and he tried to make me swap with him. I put the sixpence in my mouth to hide it and began to run, with John in pursuit, when I swallowed the coin. I was petrified. I went and told Granny McGarry and she took me to the Royal Hospital in the city, where I was checked. The doctor told her not to worry and that I would pass the sixpence in a day or two. Heading home, I asked Granny if I would have to walk fast or run to pass the sixpence and if I would still be able to buy sweets with it when it came out? I can still hear her laugh to this day.

On Owey I was known as 'Wee Margaret' as I had a cousin of the same name who was a few years older. She was called 'Big Margaret', a name by which she is still known in the family. I had five cousins on the island: Big Margaret, Grace, James, John and Mary; we were always close and are to this day.

My grandmother cooked everything on the big open fire. Later, in order to make life easier for her, my mother and her siblings got together and bought her a four-burner gas cooker hob. I was sent to the island with the cooker to show my grandmother how to use it. When the gas was connected to the cooker I turned the burners on, one by one, and lit them with a match. I repeated the drill four or five times, lowering and raising the flame on the burners so my grandmother would know how to turn them up or down. Then I asked her if she understood. I can still hear her words to this very day: 'Just leave it switched on and I will put a light to it when I need it.' Can you imagine what would have happened?

It was also on Owey Island that I met my first love, John Byrne. John's mother, Agnes, came from Owey and married a man from Aranmore Island. In the summer months John and I would meet on Owey. We would play together and I remember if anyone asked me about him I would proudly say that John was my boyfriend. He would say that I was his girlfriend. Of course we didn't even know what that meant at the time, but I knew I liked John a lot. Our paths crossed many times through our lives and in our late teens or early twenties we met and became boyfriend and girlfriend for real. So, as you can see, I had an eye for the boys from a young age!

Life was wonderful back then. There were no cares in the world. Any big decisions were made for me by my parents and I was very happy to follow the lead they gave me. I loved my parents so much and to me they were the best.

CHAPTER 2

A PLEDGE TO

MY DAD

The Promise

A man who meant the world to me
His face stays in my memory
On him I could always depend
Loyal and faithful to the end.

I remember that day he needed me
I stood beside his bed
And I fondled his head close to my breast
As parting tears he shed.

He said 'Promise me, Margaret, you will take care
Of the ones who are special to me
Your Mam will need you to help her
To raise our family.'

Not for a moment did I ever think
To Heaven my father would go
So to ease his worry, I made my promise
To the man that I loved so.

I thank our Lord in Heaven
For helping me each day
To keep the promise I made my dad
Though at times I went astray.

So rest easy dearest Father
In your home with God above
We miss you each and every day
And we all send you our love.

The day before my dad died was 15 August, the Feast of the Assumption, a holy day, when we all went to Mass. Dad didn't go that day, which was very unusual for him as he was a religious man. While I thought it was odd at the time, it never crossed my mind that it might be an indication of him being really ill. I knew he hadn't been well as I had heard him coughing a lot, and, when I think back, there were other signs that things were not normal with him.

Any time he came home from Scotland he would be out helping the neighbours. He loved our neighbour, Annie McGarvey, and would have done anything for her and her father, Josie. Josie was our local smithy; whenever I think of him, I can almost smell the scent coming from that fire and the anvil.

I remember Dad coming home one evening around that time, having been helping our neighbours, and when I met him at the back door he complained to me of being very tired. I wondered at that.

On the night of 15 August I was scheduled to sing in Fintown church hall with the band I was with then, the Keynotes; the dance would be from midnight to 2am. During that day I was in the house with my father and he asked me to sing a few songs. He even sang a few songs himself, including 'When the Fields are White with Daisies' and 'A Mother's Last Goodbye'. That night I went off to sing and when I came home I went into my mother and father's room, as I always did, even when my father was away, just to let them know that I was home. That night my dad was awake and praying with his rosary beads. He came out to me and advised me on certain things in which I could better myself. He said, 'Margaret, you have a voice given to you by God and I know you will use it well'; he also said, 'Be good to your elders and never answer back and look after your Mam because she needs you.' And he ended like he always did, 'Always remember to say your prayers.' This took place at around 5.30am. About six hours later my dad was dead.

My father was the gentlest man, a humble man and never flamboyant, a very quiet man with a great heart and everyone loved him. I never heard my father say a swear word in the seventeen years I knew him or, for that matter, heard him say anything bad about anyone. He was the youngest of the famous Doney Owen boys and all his family adored him. Whenever anyone tells me I'm very like my dad I feel very proud; my Aunty Nappy always said that to me.

My father was known to have what was called the 'cure of the evil', which seems to have dealt with quite a few problems. People would come and pray with him. I really don't remember much about the cures he had as in those days children were not allowed to sit in and be part of adult conversation, it just wasn't the done thing and we children would be put to bed. There is one memory I have of a time Dad was home from Scotland, and a local woman who had something wrong with her face arrived at the house. Dad was getting washed after doing a hard day's work cutting the turf in the bog or setting the potatoes, but of course he went and spoke with her. About a year later I was at Mass with my dad, and we met the same woman again. She and her husband spoke to us at the back of the church. My dad asked her, 'You are all clear?' and the lady replied, 'Yes, Francie, I am, and it is all thanks to you.' Since my father died I have heard many stories of the people he helped in those years. He never talked about his cures or bragged about the help he had given, it was done quietly without anyone except himself and the 'patient' knowing – that was my dad.

Once I had a growth on the middle finger of my right hand and it was so painful that it was stopping me from writing. I had it burned off by the doctor, but this didn't work and it began to weep again. Dad saw it and brought me over to his chair. He rubbed the growth for a few minutes and repeated this several times in the days that followed. After a while I noticed it was getting smaller, and then it was gone without leaving a mark. Thankfully it never came back.

People in the area would ask my dad for advice. I find it a great comfort to know that he was so very well thought of. There was a family in Kincasslagh by the name of Logue who owned the local shop, and their son, Brian, was going to be a priest – I remember Brian writing to my father asking him to pray for him and help him on his final journey towards ordination. Fr Brian Logue is someone we hold dear as a family to this day.

When Dad died so young the only reason I could think of was that maybe he was too good for this world and God had other plans for him. As I often say to people who know me well, my dad hung the moon for me and you could ask him anything. He had a way of getting a message across without having to raise his voice once.

We had two bogs in Segskinarone, near where we lived, where we saved the turf for the fire. I remember one day when I was about nine, Dad cycled to the bog and I got a lift with my neighbour Andy Logue. We lit a fire on the top bog and started working on the bottom bog. At that time Dad used to smoke and I knew there was a packet of Woodbines in his jacket pocket which he had left with our sandwiches beside the fire for when we stopped working. I had a plan. After a couple of hours in the bog, Dad told me to go up and put the saucepan on the fire so we could boil the water for tea. I saw the jacket and the packet of Woodbines in the pocket. I thought to myself that he wouldn't notice one missing so I took it and decided to hide it in a ridge in the bog. My plan was working until later when I took a pull out of the cigarette. I staggered as I inhaled the smoke, and the Woodbine was put out quickly. I called my dad a few minutes later when the saucepan had boiled and we chatted about this and that. When he had finished his sandwich and tea, he reached into his jacket pocket for the cigarettes. He smiled as he took one out and said, 'Margaret, would you like one?' He obviously knew what I had been up to. I didn't know where to look. He laughed and said, 'Don't worry, I won't tell your mother, but don't ever do that again.' I always smile when I recall that story; most children in those days would have got a good slap for doing such a thing, but not me, and not my dad.

I have never heard a bad word said against Francie O'Donnell and I am so proud to have had him as my father. He was everything you could look for in a dad and even to this day I feel that he is never far away from me. He was such a huge part in our lives and it is a shame that my youngest brother Daniel lost out on so much by not having the vivid memories of Dad the rest of us have, being so young, aged only six, when he died.

Before Dad died, a great friend of mine, Mary Bonner, was hoping to represent Dungloe at the annual Mary from Dungloe competition and she had been looking for a pearl drop necklace for her dress on the crowning night of the competition. I said that I would look for one for her as I was playing that night in Falcarragh. On my return home I had to pass by Mary's house and I thought there must be a party on as every light in the house was switched on and there were a lot of cars outside. I asked Condy from my band to stop as I had the pearl drop for Mary. But I soon discovered that it wasn't a party: Mary's father had died suddenly. There was terrible grief in the house, with everyone crying and upset. I remember saying to Mary and Rose, 'I know how you feel.' In reality I hadn't a clue how they were feeling, but I was upset because they were upset. I lent Mary a black dress with a white collar for her father's funeral, little knowing that in just six weeks I would be needing that same dress for my own father's funeral, and that I would soon know exactly how my friends were feeling.

On 16 August I went to bed after chatting to my dad after the dance in Fintown. At around 9.15am my mother called me to say that Dad was in the bathroom and not feeling well. He was asking for me. I remember going into the bathroom and there was Dad, leaning on the sink, gasping for breath. I helped him back to his room. Tears were running down his face. He said to me, 'Look at my hands, they are all white and soft.' He asked me to get his brother Dinny who lived nearby in Burtonport, and to ring his mother in Edinburgh at Aunty Nappy's, and Mam asked me to call the doctor. I remember running down to the local post office to the public phone. As I was running I realised that I had no shoes on and was wearing only a slip. I rang the doctor's number and got through to his wife. I told her what was wrong with my dad and she said the doctor would come up after his breakfast, so I ran home again. When I reached the house Mam was outside, crying, and there were a few of the neighbours in with Dad. He called for me again and asked me to kneel down beside him. He said to me that he wanted me to make a promise to him, and I recall saying, without even a thought, that I would promise to do anything he wanted. 'Look after your mam and the family,' he said. I remember saying, 'Sure how can I do that, I only earn ten shillings a night?' His response was, 'There's only one person that I can depend on that will look after them, and that is you, Margaret. Promise me.' 'I promise you, Dad,' I replied. Little did I think that this promise was going to lead to many hardships and many sacrifices for me personally, but a promise was a promise and I intended to keep it. My dad was everything to me and I know I fulfilled my promise to him the best way I could.

The doctor had still not arrived and I ran down to the post office again. However, as I was ringing him I saw his car heading up to the house. When I met him back at home I asked him what was wrong with Dad. He said that he suspected he had a punctured lung and that he was sending him to Letterkenny General Hospital for a scan as there were no X-ray facilities in Dungloe. The ambulance was in Letterkenny so the doctor took Dad in his car to Dungloe Hospital to wait for the ambulance there, and Fr Brian Logue was to bring me to Dungloe to travel with Dad on to Letterkenny. But Dad died before any ambulance arrived or indeed before I got there. A short time later a car arrived at our house. My mother went outside with my brother Daniel. A priest got out of the car; it was Fr Bonner who was the chaplain in Dungloe Hospital. My mother spoke to him for a moment and then I saw her fall to the ground, with Daniel holding on to her. I thought that Dad had got worse, but Fr Bonner changed my life with the words, 'Your dad has gone back home to Heaven.' He told us that while Dad was waiting for the ambulance in Dungloe he had asked for a priest, and that the priest had anointed him. A few seconds later Dad passed away.

My first reaction was to run. I ran and ran and ran, hoping that what Fr Bonner had said was wrong, but it was not wrong and nothing could change it. Now, I had made a promise to my dying father to help my mother raise the family and that promise I had to keep.

At seventeen years of age was I ready to be the breadwinner of the family? No, I was not. I realise that now, but back then I felt I didn't have any choice. With my hand on my heart I can truthfully say that I wanted to fill my father's shoes and take on the responsibility for my mother and my sister and my brothers. I would not let my family down. I might sometimes falter and lose my way but I would get up and start over again. I couldn't just walk away. I cared too much for each of them.

My mother was entitled to a Scottish pension as my father had worked in Scotland most of his life. In order to claim this I needed Dad's death certificate. I went to Dungloe Hospital and got the certificate from the doctor there. I then had to take it to another doctor who was in charge of the Registry of Deaths. I walked from the hospital to the house of the Registrar and asked if he could record my father's death as we needed to get the Scottish pension for my mam. He answered me sharply, saying that there were other people just as important who had to be enrolled first. I was shocked. I cried and told him that this death certificate belonged to the most important man in the world to me and we needed the money from the pension. He still refused. I walked away in tears and went across the town to Andy Logue's shop. He saw right away how distressed I was and he took me to a solicitor, Pa O'Donnell, who was also a TD. When I went back to the Registrar with Andy and Pa, he did the job immediately. I never forgot how helpful Andy and Pa were that day. Andy lives in New York now and always keeps in touch, while Pa passed away many years ago. I learnt a great lesson back then and now I always like to reach out to someone when they're down on their luck because I reckon the big people look out for themselves.

Everything seemed more difficult when Dad was gone. My mam depended on me now and I so wanted to make everything okay. As time moved on and I began having hit records as 'Margo', things got easier.

I was always able to come up trumps when anything was needed for my family, and I thank the Lord for that. Right up to her death, Mam always thanked me for the role I took, but I was proud and willing to be able to help with anything that arose within my family. I took care of all the bills that needed paying and I did it with a good heart and would do it again if I had to. The first home of our own we ever had was a council cottage and in 1973, about five years after my father passed away, I bought it outright from the council for my mam. I felt proud that day, but it was tinged with regret and a lot of sadness that my father was not around to see it happen. I know he would have been so proud to hold the key and know it was his.

At the time of my father's birth it was customary to call a child after a relative or someone close to the family. His parents had talked a lot about what my father should be called, having already used up a lot of the family names already. My grandfather was digging outside and he found a paper with a novena to 'Saint Francis of Assisi.' He brought the prayer in to his wife and they decided there and then to call the new baby Francis. When I developed a blood problem that I describe later on in this book, I was given a present of a trip to San Giovanni Rotondo in Italy to visit the tomb of Saint Padre Pio to whom I had a great devotion while I was ill, and still have. Whilst there I went to Assisi to the tomb of Saint Francis and I got a great sense of peace in my life that has remained with me to this very day.

While I was at Mass in the church where Padre Pio said his last Mass, a woman from Tipperary who was also in the congregation (she was the mother of the former Minister, Mary Hanafin) realised who I was and came and asked me if I would sing.

I felt very honoured and humbled to stand on the altar and sing where once the saint had stood before me. I felt truly blessed. I can remember each note I sang. My father too was very much aware of Padre Pio. They both died in 1968. As I stood at that altar I had my eyes closed and it really was a feeling like no other I ever experienced.

My Dad

What my father meant to me no words could ever say

Always there to listen if I ever lost my way,

So kind and understanding, a light that shone so bright

When he was gone I missed him, morning, noon and night.

To me he was my hero, the man who hung the moon

He had the greatest presence when he walked into a room

But my father was so humble, no big pomp or style

His hand reached out in friendship, yes he'd go that extra mile.

The love I felt for you, dear Dad, will never fade nor die

'Till the day I go to join you in God's home in the sky

Where we will be together, no more parting, no more pain

So rest easy, dearest Father, until we meet again.

CHAPTER 3

MY FAMILY

My mother, Julia McGonagle, came from Owey Island off Donegal's northwest coast and my dad, Francis O'Donnell, was from Acres, Burtonport, just a few miles away. They met in Lerwick off the north coast of Scotland while working in the preparation of fish for export to lands far away. Dad adored my mam, and when he used to say her name his voice grew soft with emotion. He gave her his all and he adored each of us children. After his death my mother spoke openly about her love for him and it's so sad that they did not grow old together. They gave me the values that have made me the person I am today and I thank them both for that.

I guess we are a normal, everyday family; we have our disagreements like most families, and we make up and argue again, but at the end of the day, deep down, no matter what goes on privately between ourselves, we will always be there for one another as families should be.

I love my siblings equally but if I am being honest, like most families, I guess, I am closer to certain members than to others. When I say that, it doesn't mean that if any of them needed me or was in trouble for whatever reason, I wouldn't be there; I have always been there, I would be the first in line to help. I don't agree with certain decisions that my family have made but I have to respect them and, likewise, I am sure that they are not happy with some of the decisions I have made, and I have to live with that.

When I took over my father's role, following my promise to him, I felt it was such a serious matter that to members of my family I may have appeared too forceful or over-protective, but I wanted everything to be just right for them. Many times I would panic when I feared I would fail, and today I can see I worried too much and carried the promise to my dad too far. However, I know if my family looked back and examined what I did they would realise that I did it with their best interests in mind. I had no instruction manual to guide me and even to this day I worry about my family when it really is not my problem, but I guess old habits die hard.

My older brother, John, and I are extremely close. He was the eldest of the family and I think our closeness stems from there being only two years' difference between us. It was just John and me until our sister, Kathleen, was born four years later. John is very well known for his charity work, especially his role with the mentally handicapped because of his son, Joey. John now lives in Keadue in Burtonport, two and a half miles from Kincasslagh, with his wife, Bridget, and of course my nephew and godson, Joey, who is very special to us all. John's other boy, Frankie, lives nearby with his wife and family.

No one could imagine the joy I felt the day Kathleen was born. I now had the sister that I had always wanted. I don't think Kathleen realises how proud I am of her today and always was. She is very special to me. Kathleen and her husband, John, lived at home with my mother until Mam's death. Their family have all grown up now and fled the nest.

Next to join the family was James, two years after Kathleen. James is very well known from his pub in Dublin and often when I was travelling to different parts of the world, either performing or on holidays, I would meet people who would tell me that they knew my brother. Naturally, I would assume it was Daniel, as he has become such an international name, but no, the brother they knew was Jamsie.

James and his wife, Eileen, have done very well for themselves and have a beautiful family. He owns Cassidy's pub on Camden Street in Dublin. One of his sons, Paul, lives near me in County Armagh and he, his wife and family are frequent visitors. They

Here I am with the neighbours in Donegal in the mid-fifties. I am in the front row, fourth from the right. My sister Kathleen is directly behind me and Dad next to her. Behind Dad, Mam is holding my brother James.

This is me with my brother John (Bosco). We were very close as young children, and we still are.

Here I am at ten years of age in Edinburgh when I visited my relations in Scotland with my father. This was a very special trip and I enjoyed travelling with my dad.

Aunty Nappy (left) lived in Scotland but came home sometimes to visit her family. Here we are in Donegal with her. That's Gaga, my grandmother, in the middle, with Dad on the right, and me and John in front.

Here I am with my beloved little sister Kathleen. I don't remember who owned the motorbike we're on!

My first band, the Keynotes. They were very special to me and always will be. Our wonderful travelling VW van is behind us. What fun we had travelling the roads in that van!

Allied Entertainments Limited

Here I am ready to hit the road in my car! We travelled a lot in the seventies, usually in a car with a driver, but I also liked to drive too.

Busy times as a young performer! On stage, doing publicity shots and appearing on magazine covers.

Here I am with my band the Keynotes in the early seventies. This was our last photograph together.

I made it to 'Podge and Rodge'! Here I am with the terrible duo. That was really a fun day, I can tell you.

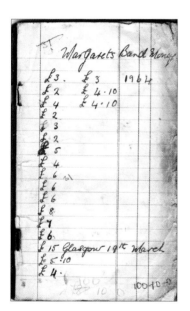

My mother kept accounts of all my earnings and my contributions to the family in my early days. I was amazed to discover later how she had noted every detail in the accounts books.

Here I am performing at RTE in my own show, 'Margo & Co', in 1972.

My great business venture, but I finally had to close it because I was too busy travelling to perform.

Donegal Person of the Year 2011 – in New York! This was such an honour, and I am enjoying it thoroughly here in the company of Rosina Gallagher (left) and Katie Barratt (right).

Here I am with my beloved nephew Joey, who has brought so much happiness to us all.

The whole family gathered for Daniel's fortieth birthday. I am in front, right, with Mam and Kathleen, and behind, left to right, there's Daniel, John and James. This was such a happy occasion.

are very special, as are all my nephews and nieces.

And then we come to Daniel, my youngest brother. Daniel was born in December 1961, ten years after my own birth. We could never have guessed what a future this little baby was going to have. I'm not going to go into Daniel's life as it is well documented in his own books and all that has been written about him all over the world, but of course he is very much part of my story, too.

Daniel started his musical career with me and my band. He had been going to college in Galway, studying to be a teacher. After a year there he announced to me that he was not going to return after Christmas, and that he wanted to sing instead. I remember being devastated as I knew by now how tough the music industry could be and I did not want my young brother going through some of the hardships I had experienced. I was worried for Daniel.

Thankfully, Daniel had really good people behind him and has become a household name in the music industry. I am very proud of him and love him dearly and am so glad that I was the person that gave the entertainer Daniel O'Donnell his first big break. Daniel tours extensively all around the world with his band now and when he is not on tour he mainly resides in Tenerife and, of course, in Donegal.

That's my family. Many times we struggled but we managed to get by together. I have wonderful memories of early childhood, both happy and sad times, when my father was absent from our lives as he had to go away to work in Scotland, but even then we always knew he would return and our home was complete again for a precious short time until he had to leave once more. I once heard Mam say when he passed on that she had been married to Dad for twenty years but that they had lived together for just thirteen months. When I heard her say that I felt so sad and thought how difficult it must have been for her and for lots of other women who had to live like that in that era.

As I look back now I realise how happy we were though we had very little. Are we happy now? I wonder sometimes if all the success has at times kept us apart. I have reached contentment in my life but as a family unit we will never have the same feeling we had all those years ago, and when I think of our family life in Donegal I feel a gentle sadness wash over me and a bittersweet sense of loving my family so much. Perhaps I should have walked away a long time ago? Maybe if I did, I would not feel the sadness I feel sometimes today. Did I do right or wrong? I often question myself, but I guess I will never know. I have had to let go of a way of life that existed only in my dreams.

So there you have us all. And the person who kept the family together was my mother, Julia, who lived to ninety-four years of age. Mam was the person who surrounded us and kept us all in line. She didn't have life that easy, being left a widow at a very young age with all the pressures that that entailed. I am just glad that I was able at least to ease the burden of financial hardship for her in keeping the promise I made to my dad.

I know that each of my siblings has their own special memories of our father. John worked side by side with him before he passed away and I will never forget how John tried to act so adult and responsible when that final day came, even though his heart was broken. Kathleen, who used to cry so much every time Dad had to go away to work, was just coming into her teenage years when he died and was devastated. James and Dad had a whistle code between them, and them alone. After Dad died, James would often go missing in the evening time and I would always find him with our dog, Rover, at Dad's grave. James left home young and went to Dublin. Daniel missed out a lot on memories of Dad simply because he was the youngest and Dad was absent in Scotland for long periods during his early childhood.

I felt so protective of them all, and still do even now that they are adults. In an odd way I still feel I need to ask their forgiveness for not being able to fill the emptiness after the loss of our dad and make the pain go away. But, on a happier note, we made it this far together and I think we have done okay. I hope we will continue to be there for one another and I am convinced that somewhere Dad, and now Mam too, are watching over us all.

Whenever things got difficult I would look to a higher power for help and know that without my faith I could not have made it on my own. There were times in my life when I thought no one was listening to my cries for help, but always, even when I was at rock bottom, somehow I was thrown a lifeline that pulled me through.

I remember one time we were having an oil range put into our house and Mam and I went to Dungloe to get the money from the bank. As we stood on the footpath outside the shop I suddenly became nervous: what if I didn't have enough money in my account to cover the cost? I looked up the street and I could swear I saw my father looking down and beckoning me to come to him. I ran towards him. I knew Dad was dead but I also know I saw him that day. When I got to the spot there was no one there. I returned to the bank and withdrew all the money I had. I was thirty pounds short. When I came out I met my father's brother, Dinnie, and his wife, Rosie, and I told them what had happened. Uncle Dinnie looked at Rosie and she said, 'Don't worry, we'll give you the money.' As they walked away I looked towards the heavens and whispered, 'Thank you, Lord' and 'Thank you, Dad.'

I often think of the meditation 'Footprints in the Sand':

One night I had a dream. I dreamed I was walking along the beach with the Lord and across the sky flashed scenes from my life. For each scene I noticed two sets of footprints in the sand. One belonged to me, and the other to the Lord.

When the last scene of my life flashed before me I looked back at the footprints in the sand, I noticed that many times along the path of life, there was only one set of footprints. I also noticed that it happened at the very lowest and saddest times in my life. This really bothered me.

I questioned the Lord about it: 'Lord, you said that once I decided to follow you, you would walk with me all the way. But I have noticed that during the most troublesome times in my life there is only one set of footprints. I don't understand why in times I needed you most, you should leave me.'

The Lord replied: 'My precious, precious child, I love you and I would never, never leave you during your times of trial and suffering. When you saw only one set of footprints it was then that I carried you.'

Anonymous

CHAPTER 4

THE KEYNOTES

My first band, the Keynotes, were the pride of many in my home county, something that made me feel very proud, too. The great belief each member of the Keynotes had in me was something I never felt with any of the other bands I had down the years. I believe it is almost like your first love or first kiss, nothing else comes close. So, to Condy, Tony, Hughie, Johnny (deceased), Paddy Joe, Francie, Eddie and Charlie, as well as the new members who came as time moved on – Martin Campbell, Johnny Cullen, Kevin Crowley and Joe O'Donnell – all of you have always had a special place in my heart.

I have so many happy memories of my time with the Keynotes,

like when we travelled down to Cavan, Galway, Mayo and further south in our bandwagon. We would have our first stop in Sligo town where we would have a meal in the Café Cairo; I loved the chicken and chips and I would always stay close to Condy, so that he would pay for my food as well as his own. Oh, yes, I was no fool and I would save my money to get another treat for myself later on!

If I hadn't lost my father in 1968 I never would have left the Keynotes; we were really starting to go places. And with them being a local band, I could still complete my education and go on to train as a nurse, as I had always intended. But I panicked because of my mam and my family, and when I was offered a secure pay packet each week to go with a different band and promoter, I really felt I had to grab it with both hands. I do believe our lives are planned ahead of us and I could see no other way at that time in my life.

My mother kept a log book of my earnings, which I still have. I sometimes look at it and think of times past. I can't turn back the hands of time but I will always have wonderful memories of my special times with the Keynotes. Whatever was special in Margo, those members in the original Keynotes saw it and took a chance on me, and for that I will always be grateful.

Our first bandwagon was a Volkswagen, but as we became more successful, Condy went to Dublin and bought a new Commer van. And when we eventually got a new red Ford Transit with our name on it, I felt so posh sitting in the front seat as we travelled to all parts of Ireland, and indeed Scotland and England. But I didn't always sit up-front. A new drummer, Johnny Cullen, joined the band and he and I seemed to get along really well. Martin Campbell and Kevin Crowley joined around that time too, but it was the drummer boy who caught my eye, so on journeys to the dances I would sit up-front but on our journey back home in the dark of night I would sit with Johnny in the back, and cuddles were always on the menu! How special the memories of those times are. I had other boyfriends, but Johnny was a little bit special.

I vividly recall our first tour in England; we sailed into Liverpool early in the morning. I knew a lot of people from home who lived in the cities we passed through and I was keeping an eye out in case I would see someone I knew. Joe McGlynn had booked us for two nights in Birmingham and the crowds were huge. From there we travelled to London, and John Greene, a man from Dungloe, had booked us for the Buffalo Ballroom in Camden town and the Gresham Ballroom on Holloway Road. John had been home in Dungloe for holidays and had come to one of our dances. On his return to London he made contact with us and booked us for our debut in that city. I will never forget the reception myself and the Keynotes received. The Buffalo later became the Carousel and I sang there many times.

I remember an incident from my first night there. I was wearing a little black jacket over my stage dress and I had a two-shilling piece in my pocket (that was my spending money for the night). I must have laid my jacket carelessly at the side of the stage and when I looked for my money to buy a mineral after the dance it wasn't there. I searched every bit of the area around where the jacket had been, but there was no money. At the time, two shillings was a lot to lose. John Greene noticed that I was upset and asked me what was wrong. When I told him my tale of woe, he put his arm around my shoulder to comfort me, then took a ten-shilling note from his pocket and gave it to me. I thought all my birthdays had come at once – a ten-shilling note was my nightly pay with the band when I started. I hugged John Greene so tight in gratitude. I knew all of John's siblings at home, indeed his brother, Michael, was the conductor on my school bus. I can still recall John's handsome face and I will always remember that ten-shilling note. The Gresham on Holloway Road had a revolving stage, something I had never seen before. The resident band played before the 'big band', and we, the Keynotes, were now the big band. As one band played off, the other band came on. I stood with microphone in hand – those old, reliable, square microphones that I loved so much – the count from our drummer was given and round we came to face the people who were hearing Margo & The Keynotes for the first time. In my eyes, we were the best. And life in show business was great, people loved what they heard and I thought then that we were destined for huge success.

A man called Tom Dolphin from near Portumna in Galway, who was working with Con Hynes Promotions, took a shine to us and helped a lot in getting us bookings, especially in the summer months. There were marquees in every townland in Ireland and he would work with Condy and Charlie McCole to fill the Keynotes' diary. We travelled to every corner of the country and it seemed that everywhere we went we left a lasting impression. My father had taught me a folk ballad called 'The Bonny Irish Boy'; I sang it for Condy and he loved it, and it became one of our favourites. Once when we went to Scotland, Condy took me to the 'Barrows' in Glasgow – a huge area with a market of barrows. I remember walking around and I heard singing coming over a loudspeaker. I followed the sound and found a stall with thousands of LPs. I asked the man on the stall who the singer was and he told me that it was an American singer called Patsy Cline. As I listened I was captivated by the voice of this singing legend. I bought three of her LPs, went back to where we were staying, found an old record player and sat, listening. I recorded many of Patsy's songs over the years but I never tried to copy the voice. I sang the songs in my own style and I think that's what was unique. Don't ever try to copy anyone, just be yourself.

It was on one of these records that I heard two songs that would be part of Margo's repertoire for the rest of my life: 'Dear God' and 'If I Could See the World through the Eyes of a Child'. Kevin Crowley did an arrangement for me of 'Dear God' as well as 'The Bonny Irish Boy', and in the weeks that followed, myself and the boys headed to the Eamonn Andrews Studio in Henry Street, Dublin, to make our first record.

There was so much excitement. Everybody in our home area

knew we were recording and wished us well; everyone was so proud of us. I recall that my dad was home at the time for the turf cutting. With our recording done we returned home in the early hours. As I always did, I went to their bedroom to let my parents know I was home. Dad reached out his arms and held me and told me he was proud of me. We all waited eagerly for the record to come out and to hear it being played on the radio. Condy went around to quite a few record labels to get them to take it on. Finally, Tom Costello, who had the Target Record Company, which was connected to Pye Records, heard something in my voice that he liked. The first time my record was to be played on the radio was on a sponsored programme at 1.45pm on Friday, 16 August 1968. This was a dream come true for me. We were all so excited, my dad more than anyone, because he had given me 'The Bonny Irish Boy'. Tragically, he died at 11.45am on that same day. My dreams were shattered and Dad never got to hear the record on air. After I left the Keynotes I never sang 'The Bonny Irish Boy' again, not even to this very day, it is just too painful.

THE BONNY IRISH BOY

His name I will not mention, in old Ireland he was born
It's true I loved him dearly but alas from me he's gone
He's gone out to America, he promised to send for me
But the face of my Bonny Irish Boy I can no longer see

I paid my passage to New York and on arrival there
To see if I could find my love I quickly did prepare
I searched New York and Florida and Boston all in vain
But the face of my Bonny Irish Boy was nowhere to be seen

Early the next morning a knock came to my door
I heard a voice I knew it was the boy I did adore
I hurried down to let him in, I never felt such joy
As when I fell into the arms of my Bonny Irish Boy

It's then that we got married and no more he'll go to sea
It's true I love him dearly and I'm sure that he loves me
It's now our first young son was born to my delight and joy
He's the picture of his Daddy and a Bonny Irish Boy
Yes, he's the picture of his Daddy and a Bonny Irish Boy.

My years spent as lead singer with the Keynotes are some of the most cherished times in my life. We travelled many miles together and cared deeply for one another. If I close my eyes I can still see all of the halls and marquees where we performed. My first St Patrick's night with the Keynotes was in 1965, in St Margaret's in Glasgow. I went shopping for the big event with Kathleen Boyle who was married to the drummer, Tony Boyle. Kathleen was one of my closest friends. The dress we chose for the St Patrick's dance was green, with matching tights and white shoes. Boy, did I look good, or so I thought. The hall was packed to capacity and when I emerged onto the stage and lifted the microphone I was in seventh heaven. Could this really be happening to me? In all my dreams I never imagined people standing by the stage just to listen to me, and then the applause as I finished my songs was the greatest sound ever. Shortly after that, a new club opened, the Marquee Club at Paisley Road, Toll, Glasgow, where the manager, big Dick Neeson, was always very kind to me and the Keynotes. As I look back now I can see why: there were 'full house' signs posted on the door every time we appeared there. I can recall playing at a victory dance when Celtic won the European Cup, I think it was 1967. The team came onto the stage with the cup and the place erupted. What a wonderful moment.

On a recent visit to Donegal I drove down the coast road from Dungloe and stopped by my grandparents' home in Acres. I closed my eyes for a while, remembering the music and song that was ever present in the Doney Owens' house. It was those people in my past who embedded the love of music in me. I continued down the road another few miles and found a little tin-roofed building known to everyone as Maggie Neil's dance hall. It was the only hall in Ireland at that time that held a dance on Christmas night – the doors opened at 12.01am and the people came from far and near. Yours Truly and the Keynotes graced the stage. We would always get a lovely meal in the house before the dance, which was also very special; in those days the band were always looked after where food was concerned. We could play to packed halls seven nights a week then.

I always had dreams about leaving home. But I wanted the decisions about when and where to be my decisions. But the reality was that there were bills at home that needed to be paid, and my promise to my late dad to look after my family left me with no choice. When the funeral was over we really had no money left for a rainy day and the bills were mounting up. I knew what I had to do. It hurts me to think that some doubted the loyalty I have or had for my family. All I will say to my family is that you had my total devotion; all I can stand accused of is caring too much and trying too hard to fill Dad's shoes, which was an impossible task.

Down through the years I have heard stories about me and my family that were so different from what actually took place, and indeed, sometimes had not taken place at all. I'm not sure whether this was idle gossip – not idle at all, actually, when it causes hurt and ill-feeling – or whether it made people feel important to seem to be 'in the know' about everything, particularly where the subject of the gossip is in the public eye. When a person gains some success everyone wants a bit of the action. Over the years I have been tried and condemned without even knowing about it. But I'm proud of all that I have achieved and all that I have done for my family. So, as they say, to hell with the begrudgers!

Sometime after my father died I was approached by three different promoters who wanted to create a new band around me, give me a recording contract and put me on the road to success. I tried to get them to take the Keynotes too, but that was not going to work, or so they told me. A hundred pounds per week in 1969, as well as a car and a driver to take me to all my engagements was a pretty good deal and a way for me to help my mother at home with the family. So I agreed to go with the promoter John McNally.

I was a very young and naive seventeen-year-old who had been sheltered and protected by the Keynotes. I was in no way pre-pared for what fate had in store for me. But there was no other way, I had to go.

Leaving the Keynotes broke my heart; the boys that made up the band were family. I didn't want to tell Condy, but I had to. Condy had believed in me since the very first night we played in Ardara in 1964 and deep down I felt I was betraying him, but things were different now and I had a family that really depended on me.

So I bade a reluctant farewell to the band, which at that time comprised Condy Boyle, Martin Campbell, Francie Diver, Kevin Crowley, Joe O'Donnell, Johnny Cullen and Eddie Quinn. We had just released our second single, 'The Road by the River' and 'If I Could See the World through the Eyes of a Child'; the dances were busy and we were now playing in Galway, West Limerick, Kerry, and even had dates in Dublin. I remember talking to my dad in my prayers and asking him to help me make the right decision. I guess I will never know whether I did or didn't. All I do know is that it would have taken the Keynotes a lot longer to achieve the acclaim that my next band, Margo and The Country Folk, got.

Just a week after giving my word to music promoter John McNally, Brian Coll arrived at my home to ask me to join him in his band, the Buckaroos. Brian was one of Ireland's greatest singers and I loved his voice; he could yodel like no other. I remember my mam had taken me to the marquee in Dungloe one summer to meet him before the dance. Pio McCann played bass guitar with Brian then; he is now a very popular DJ on Highland Radio, Donegal. I looked out our front window and saw a big maroon van with 'The Buckaroos' written in large white letters on the sides. I was so disappointed that I couldn't join Brian and Pio, but I had given my word. However, we had a great night of singing and storytelling till the wee small hours. My mother and grandmother were at home with me and I remember Granny saying, 'Isn't it a pity you promised that other man in Dublin, because you would be nearer home in Omagh than Dublin.' She really liked Brian and Pio.

Leaving my family and my beloved Donegal came at a huge personal cost. I was the loneliest person in the world, pining for home and the friends I had grown up with. I landed in Dublin on a cold evening in December 1969 and met my new manager, Johnnie Kelly. Johnnie was known for being the first man to have a hit with the song 'The Black Velvet Band' and being the drummer in the famous Capitol showband.

John McNally introduced me to the band he had formed for

me: The Country Folk. They all seemed nice, but no one could ever replace the longing in my heart for my mam, my siblings, the Keynotes and my own Donegal. All my friends were back there and that is where my heart ached to be. However, I had made my decision.

So we got stuck into rehearsals and it was sounding good, but I was desperately lonely. Communication with home was difficult. We didn't have internet, mobile phones or any of the present-day technology. And, of course, like most houses then, our house didn't have a phone.

I would finish my rehearsals and go back to the house where I had a room to sleep in. But I never warmed to this big, noisy city where I knew nobody. I longed for my home and family. After a few months I decided that I needed to get out of Dublin. I had a big job to do and I needed to succeed, but I knew if I stayed longer in Dublin, the loneliness would get worse and the job wouldn't get done.

It had to be somewhere I liked and that was practical for me to live in. When I was with the Keynotes and doing dances in Limerick and Kerry, the band and I would base ourselves in Galway in a B&B owned by Bridie and PJ Higgins. On occasions there would be no single room for me, and Art and Mary Teresa Friel, who lived next door, opened their home to me and offered me a room. Art and Mary Teresa came to all my dances when I was in the Galway area and we instantly connected. It also helped that Art was from Fanad in Donegal and I felt safe with him. When

I left the Keynotes I kept in touch with Art and Mary Teresa, and now they offered me a more permanent room as I wanted to leave Dublin.

I talked with John McNally and he agreed to the move. This proved to be a real success; it was a home away from home for me. I loved Galway, perhaps because the Connemara coast reminded me of Donegal.

My dream now was to work hard, have a hit record and make my family proud of me. It was not going to be easy. The music industry was dominated by men at the time and there were many would-be stars who had been left by the wayside when the promised success didn't come fast enough for the promoters.

So, on St Stephen's Night, 26 December 1969, Margo and The Country Folk played our first dance in Strokestown in County Roscommon. It was the beginning of what was to be a new era of success for me and for my family.

It was a rollercoaster life. We normally played five or six nights a week, with Monday off. I was also in the recording studio doing my first album. I would sometimes stop and think how different my life was to that of the friends I went around with at home in Donegal, friends like Margaret Doney (Gallagher) and Margaret Sharkey (O'Brien) who worked in Kincasslagh post office. But despite our different lifestyles, when I meet them now it's like we've never been apart, and we just pick up where we left off.

I remember a funny incident from around 1971/72 that shows how my life had changed. I was dating a really nice Irish guy who was working in London. I was just out of hospital after having my appendix removed and I had a little time off. My boyfriend was arriving from England so we could spend some time together. I was meeting him in Sligo and heading for Donegal. I started out pretty early and, as I had time to kill in Sligo, I decided I would go into the Great Southern Hotel beside the station. I went into the dining room and, boy, was it posh. I was handed a menu and I decided to have a *filet mignon*. The waiter arrived with what I would call a deep pan and proceeded to cook my meat close to the table; I had never seen food cooked like this before. There was a jug of water on my table from which I poured myself a glass. When the filet was almost ready I saw him throw brandy on the steak in the pan and it went up in flames. I jumped up and threw my glass of water on the pan to put out the fire. I said to the waiter, 'You are lucky I was here. The whole place could have gone up.' The waiter just looked at me and said, 'Margo, that's what it is supposed to do.' Everybody was laughing and I felt so embarrassed. It is a true saying – you can take the girl out of the country but you can't take the country out of the girl.

Getting back to where we were, Margo and The Country Folk were in big demand everywhere. So many people had emigrated and because I leaned a lot towards the Irish ballads I think I was a link to home with all the people who had left their native soil. Thousands of my records were sent overseas. I guess I didn't really understand how popular I was fast becoming. Certainly, success didn't change me one bit as I didn't get caught up in all the glitz of show business.

The songs I sang were mainly about Ireland, and also old Country music. I still sing them today and they will be sung fifty years from now when I will be only a memory, but I hope that Margo, the singer from Donegal, will have left her mark on Country and Irish Music.

CHAPTER 5

THE ONES WHO

GOT AWAY

I am just an ordinary woman with the same dreams and feelings as everyone else. I have had lots of heartache in my life. I have also lost the loves of my life over and over again. Time and time again I would think: this time it will be okay, this time I will find who and what is right for me. But as another relationship ended, I would often say, why me? The truth is, why not me?

I guess I became a fascination to many as my life was out there in the public eye – especially as I wanted to keep my private life exactly that: private. I did not mix in show-business circles and once or twice I have even been referred to as a sort of recluse.

It may have been my life plan to marry and settle down with the man of my dreams, but it was never meant to be. With my kind of life it was difficult to meet someone and have a normal man-woman relationship. I was always on the road and up there on the stage. I wasn't able to meet a fellow and have a normal courtship. I had wedding bells in sight a couple of times, but I lost those chances of marriage and having a family. Today I can hold my head up and take full responsibility for the things I wished might happen but never did.

A lot of times I put the worry about Mam and the promise I made to Dad ahead of anything I would or could do. Can I explain why? No, I can't. I just did. In show business it is hard, sometimes, to be sure of what is real and what is not real.

I'm not one for blowing my own trumpet but I am a God-fearing person, like most, and I am a kind person. I sure have faults and they are many. I can sometimes be too outspoken, but that's me, I can't change what I am no more than the next person.

I don't mind people asking me questions; I would much rather they did that than make assumptions about me and my life without knowing the facts. Being Margo had its own personal cost when it came to love; the more popular you were the more rumours you would hear. I never really handled the rumours at the time, although they can damage you and leave you with low self-esteem. Maybe I felt that reacting to them could cause even more damage? In this chapter I deal with some of these rumours in a way that I have never done before.

I remember playing in Donegal town one night in the famous Pavisi Ballroom when I was with the Keynotes, and even at that tender young age the rumours had started. I heard a story going around that I was pregnant; I was totally shocked. I wasn't pregnant and started to wonder had I put on a lot of weight or something? It just wasn't the done thing in those days to get pregnant out of wedlock in rural Ireland and if you did, it was considered very shameful for the family. At that particular time I was doing a steady line with Johnny Cullen, the drummer in the Keynotes.

Because of my profession it wasn't that easy to meet boys. When I was at the dances obviously I would be on stage singing, and there were less chances to have a chat with boys. When you did meet someone it wasn't on a normal basis as I was working all the time and things were awkward, but I had my fair share of boyfriends. The first boyfriend I had was from Annagry, followed by a guy I met in Scotland but who now lives at home in Donegal, and of course I went out with Johnny Cullen from Letterkenny, one of the boys in the band in my earlier years.

Going back to rumours, they will always exist when a person is in the public eye. A lot was said about me in the past and I did not deny or confirm things that I was supposed to have done or said. Today I wonder if I should have taken a different approach, but I wonder what would I have gained? My life as I have lived it has been very simple, but sometimes I would find myself worrying about what was being said about me. Everyone has loved and lost in their lives, including me.

Things in my life have largely been just black and white. The rumour of me having children and giving them up for adoption was one that gained a lot of credence; people even had the name of the person who had adopted them! Where these wild stories came from I swear I will never know but, believe me, if I had been lucky enough to have had children they would be with me forever.

Going back to rumours, though, my sexuality too has been questioned on several occasions, both by people I know and by people I have never met and never intend to meet. I will tell you that I have many friends whom I love dearly, both male and female. I openly tell them that I love them, whether it be on a birthday card or Christmas card, or in conversation. I will tell them I love them and appreciate them. I have many friends who are straight and many who are gay and I love them all equally. They all have been special in their own way. I guess I have come to be content with who I am today and don't feel I need to be in a relationship or have a partner. I'm just happy being me.

Rumours about being pregnant or having children were to continue throughout my life, including that I was actually Daniel's mother rather than his older sister – this, despite the fact that there are only ten years' difference between us in age, so it would have been classed as something of a miracle if I were his mother! Where these rumours start makes one wonder – and who starts them and why they start them. Daniel was beginning to get really popular back then and had a very clean image. Perhaps someone wanted to taint that, or maybe get at me through him, or vice versa? I don't really know, but if I was his mother I would have openly admitted it. I always felt so sorry for our mother at that time because I felt she could be hurt by this rumour more than Daniel or me.

I remember hearing a story where a well-known TV personality and his wife had adopted two children who were supposed to have been mine. Not alone that, but the rumour went that when I was doing a photo-shoot in the area where this family lived, I wasn't there for a photo-shoot at all, really, but to visit my two children! It's amazing how this sort of gossip becomes accepted as fact and then people add to it and add to it until the reality becomes completely blurred. As for me, because I knew the rumour was totally false I didn't even bother to check whether the couple had adopted children or not.

On a serious note, though, I wish I had a child. I love children and if I were young today I would have a child with or without having a husband. The path I longed for in life was to be a nurse, get married, have children and live happily together, but that was not to be.

In truth, I could fill a book with the rumours I have heard about myself and the relationships I am supposed to have had. I know how many relationships I had in my life and with whom; I don't feel I have to explain myself to anyone. I was in love with a wonderful boy from my home county and when I fell in love I fell hard. As you know I liked to dream and this time it was no different. I had a dream, this one I was sure would come true and I was ready to leave the stage behind, get married and settle down, but it wasn't meant to be. My family always came first every time and today I know what I didn't know then, that this was the main reason why we parted.

I never wanted to feel that heartache again and it was a long time before I let anyone get close to me, but time passed and I did. In 1978, just shortly before I was to be married to my then boyfriend, I was handed a letter from him, delivered to me by my brother James. Basically it said he wasn't ready to settle down. Once again I felt lost and wondered 'why me?' It took longer this time for me to try again. My last serious boyfriend was a wonderful guy named Tony Tracy, who was in the music business. We went out together, split up, got back together, both feeling all along that someday we would make it, but it wasn't meant to be. Tony, a wonderful singer and guitarist, lost his fight against cancer on 28 February 1989. His passing broke my heart. When I think of Tony I realise he had a nature very like my father's. After that my life remained pretty empty in the relationship sense, but occasionally I would go out with others.

I never did seem able to let go of the fact that my family needed me and needed the money that I was bringing in through my singing. Anything I myself wanted to do had to take second place; perhaps the feeling was a comfort zone and I was at ease with the feeling of being needed, or maybe I had a fear of the unknown and every time I was close in another relationship I panicked and another dream ended.

Finally I did not want to pick up the pieces of my heart again. I realised all I wanted in my life was contentment and a kind of peace. I have let life run its course and go where it takes me. I have wonderful friends, both male and female, and I am content in my life. Am I sad that I loved and lost? Yes, I am, and I wish I had married and had a family, but for many reasons it just didn't happen.

I accept who I am today and where I am. I could cry and feel sorry for myself, but I won't do that. The love of my life, or loves of my life, are gone – yet even now there are sometimes rumours. But I walk proudly on with my memories and with my friends.

CHAPTER 6

SUCCESS OVERNIGHT
WITH THE COUNTRY
FOLK

T he wonderful musicians who came together to interview for a place in Margo and The Country Folk were all so talented that soon we were ready to launch this new band under the slogan 'The Sound of the Seventies'. Looking back on it now, I don't think I allowed myself to fully enjoy the great period around the birth of the band because I was still upset at having to leave the Keynotes.

The crowds that came to see our shows were quite unbelievable. Remember that, unlike today, the scope for advertising was limited to newspapers, postering or radio. But we were lucky that it was boom-time for the showbands, with ballrooms and marquees in practically every town in the country, as well as lots of music festivals. And in every town and dancehall there seemed to be a character or two, sometimes more, and we all looked forward to meeting up with these special folk who became like family to us.

Dublin had dancing every night of the week. There were dancehalls in every part of the city: the National, the Ierne, the Town and Country, the Irish Club, the Crystal, the Olympic and the Tara, to name but a few of the better-known venues. The National Stadium also hosted concerts. The people who managed these great venues built up great friendships with us artists down through the years.

It was an era that took me to another level. I sang on all the great stages and this exposure brought the voice of Margo into the homes of Irish emigrants all over the world. I went from being known parochially to being recognised by almost everyone I met, both nationally and internationally. But I came from a very grounded background and seemed, at that time, to take it all in my stride.

The success of Margo and The Country Folk was unreal. Everybody wanted us. This went mostly over my head. I was being paid £100 per week and I just felt I had to earn it, so I worked hard.

I loved singing, and every night in different places I would meet new people who loved what Margo had in her voice. I thank God every day for the wonderful gift that was given to me.

We toured from Cork to Donegal, all over the West of Ireland, to Dublin, Killarney, and every corner of Ireland. The crowds came and loved what they saw and heard. I don't believe it's all about being a great singer, it's the full package. You have to connect with the people and I found myself totally at one with my fans; they grew with me and I grew with them, and it was wonderful. I recall one night when I was singing in the town hall in Killarney and the crowd was so huge they took the doors off so more people could see the show. I have a friend who is one of the top DJs on Kerry Radio who stills talks about that night.

We had enormous success in England too, with Irish emigrants turning up in droves in the ballrooms of every major city. And, of course, because I was from Donegal, our popularity was guaranteed in Scotland, where so many of those from my native county lived and worked.

I could never have prepared myself for the explosion of Margo and The Country Folk. In every magazine and newspaper that had show-business features, there I would be as Margo. When you turned on the radio stations, Margo and The Country Folk would be playing. It was surreal. Sometimes it felt as though I was out of my own body as Margo, and Margaret O'Donnell was somebody else! You will notice how I often refer to myself as Margo, as if she is a different person because sometimes she seems like that. It's even hard at times to say who is writing this book – Margo or Margaret O'Donnell. One thing I am sure of, though, Margaret O'Donnell owes a great deal, as does my family, to Margo. Without Margo things would have been a lot different, and I can honestly say I will never, ever forget the people who helped me get there.

When we were playing at home in Ireland, the car would arrive each evening for me at Art and Mary Teresa's house in Galway and it would take me to the four corners of Ireland. I can tell you the crowds were enormous in those days. So much so that if a band didn't get large numbers of people at the halls in some places you would not be invited back. I just loved going to the different venues, whether it be the Traveller's Friend in Castlebar in County Mayo, the Mount Brandon Hotel in Tralee, County Kerry, Pontoon in County Mayo, or Clonakilty and Bantry in County Cork. Singing to the crowds was just something special and I loved it. I don't believe that the overnight success I experienced with Margo and The Country Folk could be achieved today.

The money that was being made by promoters and others involved in the industry was incredible for the time. Probably like most performers on a fixed salary, I never received a penny more than my wage, but I was grateful for that wage. A percentage of our earnings from our shows was put away for recordings and publicity, so essentially I and the band made the money to pay for everything. But I felt that as my money went to my mam and the family I was pleased and very proud to be able to look after them. Then there were the recordings, which I paid for, but never received any royalty. I knew I deserved something from my records, though I didn't know what exactly, but I was afraid to rock the boat – it was easier to just go along with everything. When I did pluck up the courage to start asking questions I was told that all the extra money went on publicity and recording. I said I thought that the percentage put away from the shows should take care of those things. I also said that it seemed like I was paying for everything – and I was told to be quiet or I'd be sorry, with those words the matter rested. Income tax was another problem. I paid tax every week and I thought it was all taken care of, but years later I found out nothing had been paid over and in later years I had to pay money to the Revenue that was owed since 1970; I met with the tax people and sorted it out as best as I could. Although I was selling more records in Ireland in the 1970s than the Beatles, I was not getting rich on the proceeds. But when I had my very first No.1 record, 'I'll Forgive and I'll Try to Forget' in 1970, my wages were increased from £100 to £200 per week.

Whatever about money, I have to say that I get huge pleasure when I am told how much Margo meant to people. Even today, people will come up to me and tell me how my songs and my voice enriched their lives, and it's such a gift to think that I was able to bring a bit of joy and cheer to others.

When I joined John McNally's organisation all those years

ago, I was signed to ARA Records, which had links with EMI Records that had their base in Manchester Square, London. In those days you would record twelve songs at a time and I remember flying to London on a few occasions to get the songs done. Instead of one musical arranger, there would be three, as they wanted the songs to be differently arranged. Bob Barrett from EMI produced all my records in those days and I recorded in Abbey Road where, of course, the Beatles recorded – in fact, they were once recording in the studio next to where I was recording. They were huge at that time, but this didn't faze me: I remember Bob often taking us to a little bistro down the road for lunch, and on one occasion the Beatles were there and I was introduced to them. We had no mobile phones in those days to take a picture and I didn't carry a camera at that time so I have no photo to remind me of the meeting. They seemed lovely people, despite their huge success. What some people fail to remember is that these personalities are just like you and me, ordinary people who came into the world the same way as us and will leave this world the same way. Of course, some do let it go to their heads and I feel sad when I hear of certain celebs today acting as though they are above everyone else and forgetting who put them where they are, but I guess they will learn their lesson soon enough.

The wonderful outpouring of love for me from the fans was not just confined to Ireland or England. In 1972 I went on my first tour of America. It was March and I had just finished a fourteen-night tour of England, ending on St Patrick's night in the famous Galtymore in Cricklewood, London. Sadly, the Galtymore is gone now, but it lives on in the memory of all those thousands of couples who met and fell in love there; indeed, many had their wedding there. It's a great pity to lose history, and the Galtymore was steeped in the history of our emigrants who found comfort and links with their homeland within the four walls of this great dancehall. But back to my American tour. I landed in JFK airport at around 6.30pm on a Wednesday evening and there were quite a number of people there to meet me. I was travelling with Sean Brogan, a wonderful guy who worked for my office. Marie and Oliver Bracken were there, and another Margaret O'Donnell, a family friend from near my home in Donegal. Marie Bracken was my cousin, and although she was born and bred in New Jersey she was Irish to the core. Her husband, Oliver, hailed from County Offaly and was a cop in New Jersey. During the tour I stayed with Marie and Oliver while Sean was just down the block (as they say in America) with Margaret O'Donnell. Marie and Oliver did me proud. The night I arrived they hosted a party in my honour, and I met many cousins that I never even knew I had.

On the Friday night I was singing in the Tower Ballroom in Queens. The promoter was Bill Hartigan from County Leitrim. Before I went on stage he told me that the people loved Country music as well as Irish. I stepped on stage and sang two old-style Country songs, then the crowd began shouting for 'Glenswilly', 'Shanagolden – or any Tipperary town'. I knew right away what these people loved Margo for: the songs that brought them memories of home in Ireland. It was a feeling like no other, singing the songs I loved to people who loved me. Margo had arrived. The next night I was in the Red Mill in the Bronx and in the Jaeger House. The crowds were huge; it was standing room only and the reception we got was just incredible. I felt so at home. Emigration was at its peak at that time and I met so many people that I knew. From there it was on to Boston, Chicago, Philadelphia, Detroit, and the crowds still came. It was a wonderful, wonderful tour.

When I boarded the plane to go back to Ireland I felt I had climbed a huge mountain and lived to tell the tale, and what a lovely tale it was. I arrived back in Dublin early in the morning and got a few hours' sleep. Then, at 6pm it was time to fly off again, this time to London to appear at the International Country Music Festival in Wembley. On the bill were Loretta Lynn, Conway Twitty, Dottie West and Tom T Hall, to name just a few. I felt I was a real jetsetter and I loved it. When you're young it all seems easy and it was no bother to me to cope with all the demands. Whenever I am asked what it was like back then I say that it was an era like no other and it will never be like that again. I am so glad I was part of it all and I will hold onto my memories forever.

Both at home and abroad I was enjoying huge success and Margo and The Country Folk topped the bill at the Royal Albert Hall in London as well as the National Stadium in Dublin. In later years we went to Carnegie Hall in New York. I have been blessed to meet so many wonderful entertainers throughout those years, including the late great Johnny Cash, Glen Campbell, Hank Locklin, the Statler Brothers, Slim Whitman, The Beatles, Dolly Parton and many others, either recording or touring with them. And, of course, I met our home talents such as Big Tom, Philomena Begley, Susan McCann, Larry Cunningham, Dermot O'Brien, Brian Coll, Gene Stuart, my brother Daniel, and almost all the Country artists in Ireland. I performed at all the music festivals, including at Wembley Stadium with Loretta Lynn and Conway Twitty. Those were the days.

If I were to say honestly what the highest and most important achievements for me at that time were, the things that spring to mind are: when I got the No. 1 spot in the Top Twenty with the single 'I'll Forgive and I'll Try to Forget', and receiving the Girl Singer of the Year Award – and the welcome I received from my own people when I returned to Donegal after it.

I remember the day I was named Girl Singer of the Year like it was yesterday. My sister, Kathleen, and her friend, Brid, and I drove from Galway to Donegal town, hitting the road to Glenties. Kathleen knew that there was going to be a surprise party for me to celebrate the occasion. When we reached the grotto in Glenties on the road to Dungloe there was a cavalcade of cars all across the road to bring me home for the party. The scene was extraordinary. In those days, cars were not that common in Donegal and to see all the people from home queuing to see me in the village hall that night made me feel that I was extra special. Although I had performed all over the world at very prestigious places and had received many awards, I think to be recognised by the people at home was the highest honour I could get.

Television played a big part in my life and my appearance on the 'Late Late Show' in 1969 really had a huge effect on my career. Not long afterwards I was asked to host my own television programme on RTÉ, called 'Margo & Co'. Then Margo and The Country Folk changed their name to Margo & Co – this followed my first six weeks of my television show. Some personnel also changed – we revamped the band and brought back brass instruments again; I had two tenor sax players, Davy Traynor and Jim Malone from Dublin, they also played baritone saxophone and clarinet. Ray Doherty from Derry was on guitar (lead), Joe Murray from County Meath was on keyboards and accordion – Joe was also a great singer. Paddy Higgins was my drummer – he was from Galway – and Frank McCaffrey from County Mayo was on bass guitar. Frank went on to become such a popular recording artist and is one of my favourite singers.

I have so many memories of places I have been to and the people I have met. I know the people who are important to me and they know who they are. However, there are many who made life better for me who don't know that they did. For example, I often think of Bill Sherlock from Moygara in County Sligo, who I used to buy my cars from in the 1970s. He always made sure I had a safe car as I travelled the roads of Ireland. I am still friendly with his son Gerry. Bill and his wife, Mary, were great friends to me, hardworking country people, with hearts of solid gold. On the day I would arrive in Moygara to collect a new car there would be great excitement, as Margo was coming to town! Bill would set to work getting my new purchase ready. He did all the checks and tests himself and would explain everything to me so that I would feel secure when driving the vehicle away. Mary would make sure the kettle was on the boil and would feed me well before I left their family home.

I was not without admirers and I got loads of lovely letters from men proposing marriage. My fan club at the time was looked after by Doreen. I would spend time once a month checking through the fanmail, but if anything needed prompt attention in between, Doreen would let me know. Strangely, a lot of the marriage proposals came from farmers who seemed to think that I would make a great farmer's wife – I can honestly say, without hesitation, that I would have been a useless liability where farming was concerned!

Others would tell me how my singing kept them company at work. They would listen to it on tractors, lorries, and everywhere you can think of. And I really loved the carnivals with the huge marquees out in the fields in the country at the time – it was a way of touching the hearts of country folk. When I am travelling somewhere nowadays and I pass little villages where I sang, I can point to the field that hosted some of the greatest music events in past times. I recall, as I know others can too, that there were no dressing-room facilities for changing your clothes – we changed in fields – and no mod cons of any kind. The bandwagon would pull into the field beside the tent in the late evening and the local children would gather around for autographs. These kids heard nothing but our music in their homes and seeing the people who sang those songs was so exciting to them. There was nothing like the feeling I got from the fans when I stepped up on the stage. It was a love so special, no words could explain it.

I will always remember the era of Margo and The Country Folk and Margo & Co – the success we had, the people we met, the places we performed, and the popularity we had at that time was like no other. However, things were to take a downward turn, and I was to succumb to an evil I had never known before.

CHAPTER 7

THE DARKNESS THAT ALMOST STOLE MY SOUL

I am really grateful for what I have achieved in my life. I know I could have achieved more, but I won't beat myself up about that. If I had walked an even pathway and not given in to the demons, I know I could have more – but I am what I am and I have what I have, and regrets are a waste of time. I have travelled on a great journey and I have more to travel, I hope, in the time to come.

The descent into darkness began quite early on in my career and slowly began to engulf me – and I wasn't even aware of it when it started to happen. I was able to ease people's lives with my voice and the songs I sang – songs of emigration, heartache and loss, among others – and so many people were inspired, for which I am grateful. But I did not have the ability to help myself during my darkest days. What caused this darkness? It began in the difficult times after leaving the Keynotes and my family in Donegal, at the period when Margo came into her own in the music business. I felt very alone and I didn't know who to trust in the business. I had no one to rely on. I have never discussed this aspect of my life with anyone, except in therapy with my counsellor in Aiséirí many years later.

And in 1971 I was involved in a motor accident when travelling between Killarney and Castleisland in County Kerry which caused me problems. Afterwards I started to have blackouts. I went to a doctor who prescribed medication. After singing one night, I felt dizzy and had one of my blackouts and as I was coming round, this man, whom I knew, was performing a lewd act in my presence and though I was never physically raped, I was forced to perform a sex act on this person. Abuse can take many forms and this event affected me very badly. Although nothing like that ever happened to me again, that one instance left me feeling dirty and with very low self-esteem. I couldn't sleep and was prescribed sleeping pills, which I took for a long time to blot out these horrible memories that raged inside me.

In the early 1970s it was suggested by a certain person in show business that if I sexually obliged him I would get further in my career. I ran so scared I wanted to die. I believe that sort of thing happens right up to the present day, but I am proud to say I never slept my way to the top. I made it with the help of the wonderful public who have always supported me and without giving my pride and dignity to anyone. I feel that no one should have to stoop to this level to get on in their life. Today when I hear of abuse I realise that perhaps I was lucky to have escaped with what happened to me the night of my blackout, but I will never forget it. Now I feel I am over the trauma, but I needed to put it in this book in order to get that closure.

Margo and The Country Folk were constantly at the top of their game. Everybody wanted us everywhere and, inevitably, the stress began to build up. But I felt sure that I could handle all that was going on around me. We were doing shows six and sometimes seven nights a week then, and any free time was spent in the recording studio working on my first LP, which consisted of twelve songs, a mixture of Irish and Country. I was always referred to as 'The Queen of Country & Irish' and Philomena Begley was known as 'The Queen of Country'. We both tease each other about that even to this present day.

However, I was trying to deal with loneliness, I hated being away from Donegal, I missed my friends so much and of course I missed one man in particular: my father. Each year, from the end of July to 16 August, Dad's anniversary, I would be so down within myself that I felt I was smothering. Each year that period felt as though it was getting longer, the clouds were getting lower and darker and it was getting harder and harder to deal with.

In 1974 things got worse for me. I was on my way to sing at the Corofin Carnival in Galway when I was involved in another car accident. On a rainy Friday night, 19 July, I was driving along and passing a pub called the Trapper's Inn outside Galway city, when a car came out of the car park and drove straight into me. I knew nothing until I came around in the Galway Regional Hospital. I had severe head injuries, broken bones and a lot of facial scarring. It looked at one stage that Margo might be no more. It was just terrible and as a result I was off the road for almost twelve months. Before the accident I had moved into an apartment on my own, quite close to my good friends Art and Mary Teresa. One day I got a taxi from my apartment to the hospital for my check-up as I wasn't able to drive myself. The results of the check-up were not very good. When I was coming home I asked the taxi man to drop me off at Ryan's Hotel on the Dublin Road. I went in and sat in the foyer. I was now twenty-three and up to this stage of my life I was a Pioneer – I had never broken the abstinence pledge taken at my Confirmation and didn't even know what alcohol tasted like. I recalled hearing someone asking for a vodka and orange, so I asked the bartender could I have a vodka and orange. I knew the man well and he looked at me funnily, as I would normally have had an orange juice or a Coke.

I had the drink and it didn't feel too bad. I was on crutches at the time and not able to get about too well. But I needed more than metal crutches. I was so lonely and down that I needed something to prop me up. When I realised that alcohol didn't make me feel too bad I thought that would be my crutch. I ordered another vodka and orange and it seemed as if things were getting easier. In hindsight this was the worst decision I made in my life. I became good friends with the demon alcohol. It almost destroyed me. I was also on a lot of prescribed medication at the time for my injuries, including an anti-depressant, and I never realised the damage medication could do when mixed with alcohol.

When I was off work after my accident I worried about my mother and felt I had let my family down. When I should have been thinking about myself and how to recover, I was wracked with worry about other people. I was also desperately lonely, and living alone didn't help. If I had had someone to tell my fears to, it would not have been so bad. Out of fear and worry I started to build a monster inside me, and it seemed as if part of who I was would be destroyed by this monster. I never took drugs, apart from those that were prescribed for me. I thought it was okay if a doctor gave them to me, but oh, how wrong I was.

I wobbled through that year and my first gig after the accident was just before Christmas in the Royal Albert Hall in London. I was terrified. I didn't have any confidence. I had scarring on my face – not an awful lot – but to me it was hideous. Deep down I just wanted to run and keep running. Mick Clerkin from

Release Records, now known as Rosette Records, a decent guy who always treated me fairly, was doing the concert with me in London. I couldn't get my head around it, everything was just different and my fear of playing had got a lot worse. I travelled over on the plane with Mick. I took a couple of tablets and had a drink and I felt fine then. I felt that I got through the show quite well, but I didn't realise that when I drank my words would be slower; I couldn't change key in the songs as quickly either. I didn't see or hear any of that, but I had found something that took the fear of the stage away and that was all that mattered to me then because when I had thousands of people looking up at me in my concerts I now felt a fear like no other, I was just petrified.

Alcoholism is a cunning disease. People I knew didn't want to tell me what a mess I was, in case of hurting my feelings. Believe me, people did notice that Margo wasn't on top of her game. Perhaps people felt sorry for me. On what was the start of my downward spiral, I wouldn't have a drink every day or every night, or even when I went out at times. I drank in stages. A fear would build up of something that was far in the future, maybe a big show, recording an album, or maybe, if I'm being honest, having to meet some of the people in the business that I was dealing with. When I had to deal with these people or these events I would have a drink and then I would not be afraid. That continued for almost twelve years. I saw several doctors during that period and received varying advice. They told me to take this pill or that pill, but none of them worked. I attended some AA meetings but that didn't work for me either. All seemed to add to the confusion inside of me.

There are so many different ways of being an alcoholic. I'm a very addictive person, perhaps it's in my genes. I knew I needed to smarten up my show but after the shows there was always someone to hand you a drink, always a bar open and always a way of getting a drink when I wanted it. But I have to take the responsibility for all of that. If I had one drink it was noticeable. Drink had an instant effect on me. The demon was frightening. It got so much of a grip on me that it made me unsure of who I was.

I hid drink from everyone, not only from my family. But my mother found out that I was drinking and as drink was never something she was happy about, it must have been difficult for her to understand. My family would have only seen a tenth of what was actually going on. My name became associated with people I never knew and with places I had never been. My credibility was at an all-time low. I was being blamed for things that I had no part in. I heard awful things about myself. I walked into conversations where performers were talking about me. I was good gossip. I still remember who those people are. When I was at the end stages of trying to give up drink, a person in show business actually handed me an alcoholic drink. Thankfully, I didn't take it, but I never had much respect for that person again.

After one year off the road I returned to the stage a very unsure nervous person. I came back under management of Release

Records, whose top man was Mick Clerkin, whom I mentioned already. Mick formed Country Pride around me and I shared the stage with Mattie Fox from Longford. I toured for a while but I was not feeling good, and I was in a bad place in my mind. I decided I would step down from the ballrooms and thought maybe cabaret would suit me better, but after a few weeks Mick Clerkin got myself and Larry Cunningham together in the studio to record a duet called 'Mr. Peters'. Such was the success of 'Mr. Peters' that Mick suggested Larry and myself joined forces as Larry-Margo and The Country Blue Boys, who were originally Larry's band. It was unreal how popular this marriage of two singers was – I suppose neither of us really needed the other, but it was a wonderful time and I have fantastic memories of our time together.

We recorded a duet album aptly called 'Mr. Peters', and it was a bestseller and everyone was happy. But soon I noticed unease and speaking to the band personnel I found out they were unhappy, and so – whether it was the right or wrong thing to do – the boys and I left Larry and became Margo and the Blue Ridge Boys. There was no rancour between Larry and me, and Larry continued singing, and was as popular as ever, until his death some time ago. I got to spend some time with him and his wife, Beatrice, before his untimely death and we were getting ready to celebrate a tribute night in Larry's honour. He phoned me and suggested we re-unite and sing 'Mr. Peters' on the night, but, alas, he became ill. That plan was not God's plan and Larry was called home. I have recorded his big hit, 'Lovely Leitrim', in his memory and I hope that wherever he is watching us from, he has all the happiness he deserves.

While I was touring with Larry the lead guitar player caught my eye. His name was Tony Tracy – I have mentioned Tony already, but if I hadn't joined Larry I might never have known Tony. Both of them are gone now and I just know if there is great music in heaven, Tony and Larry will be part of it. May they both rest in peace.

In 1978 I bought the Viking House Hotel, near home in Donegal. It had been run successfully by Fred and Minnie Bilberg for many years. They decided to retire and with a hopeful heart I purchased it. The manager was a lovely man called Pat O'Shea, from Killorglin in County Kerry, and we worked together for two seasons. I was very busy on the road with my band at the time and it was proving too stressful to juggle both. One had to go, so, reluctantly, I gave up the Viking House.

In the late 1980s I felt I couldn't take anymore and I had to get my life back on track. I had lost my life savings in a financial investment. I was very lonely and I was drinking. I went to the doctor and asked to be referred to a specialist. Two weeks later and on the eve of going to the specialist, I felt so alone that I rang the Samaritans. I was at rock bottom.

I saw the specialist the following week. The male specialist was on holiday so I was seen by a woman, Dr McInerney, and that really was when my life started to turn around. I can recall it as if it was yesterday. I so wanted to get better and I wanted to get away from always feeling sad and lonely. My heart was broken at how lonely I had become and how nothing mattered in my life.

As soon as I met Dr McInerney I knew that she was not someone I could fool easily. She had a wonderful way of looking at things, she didn't judge me or take out a book to write a prescription. She listened to what I had to say and gave what I now know was great advice. I left that day with another appointment to see her. My steps were lighter and I felt more positive, a feeling I hadn't felt for a long time.

Shortly after that Dr McInerney notified me that she wanted me to go to a private hospital in Galway to be medically checked out. On my way to the hospital I decided to have one final drink. I went into the Imperial Hotel in Eyre Square and then on to the hospital. I'm not sure if it was the way I talked to her or smiled, but I will always remember her quietly saying to me, 'Did you enjoy that drink?' I knew then that I wasn't going to be able to fool this woman – not indeed that I wanted to fool my doctor, but I liked to be one step ahead, or so I thought.

I do believe that my luck and my life changed that day. It was a slow process; I did not get well quickly. I believe I was a big challenge but when I was getting my feet on solid ground again my doctor was so happy for me and every time I struggled she could sense it. But I knew she would not give up on me.

I didn't come out of the darkness in one clean sweep but I

started to regain my confidence. It was much more difficult than I ever thought it would be. It was painfully lonesome, heartbreaking and terribly frightening coming from the dark of that life and into the clean and sober world that I live in today. I do believe it was the good Lord that sent that doctor into my path and I want to say thank you to her for her help and support in giving me back what was lost in my life for so long.

I felt like I had to learn to do everything again. It was like I was born again and life took on a whole new meaning. I had forgotten how to be happy. I was always so sad and as I always tried to hide the fact that I drank, I spent most of the time alone. However, it was not always alcohol that made me appear like that. I was often under the influence of some prescribed pill or other. I was pretty much in a mess, but I knew I had to say goodbye to the awful life I had or I wouldn't be alive today.

I never talked to Mam or my family about my problems as I really felt I had to be the strong one. I felt I just couldn't tell them as I would be letting them down and I felt I had to lead the way. There were many times I wished my family would rescue me from this life of pure hell that I was going through but I couldn't ask them for help. Maybe when they read this they will realise how much I needed them to help me out of the darkness that almost stole away my soul.

I meet people who ask me how I got over the bad times to be where I am right now. I hope I can explain that a little, and maybe if any person reading this feels that they are where I was, then I know the first thing I had to do was admit that I was powerless, and that addiction, from whatever source, had beaten me. I had tried many short cuts to regain normal sanity in my life but now I realise that the short cuts don't work. I wanted to get my life back so I would not be an embarrassment to all of my family, but that was so wrong as I felt I had to do it for someone else – like my mother, or my brother Daniel, who was embarking on a successful career in the music business. It took me a long time to realise that I had to do it for me and me alone.

The dawn of that realisation was the start of my long journey back to normality and to where I find myself today. I must add that each person's road is different and the route and journey I travelled may not suit another person, but it will be similar and the goal is to achieve the same end result. It really is one day at a time and no day is easy; it's a lonesome journey on which there is much pain.

Quite recently I had a bad experience and I spoke to a friend about it. After we had discussed it, my friend asked me, 'Margo, were you tempted to drink at all?' I was able to answer without hesitation, 'Absolutely not.' Once I had answered and knowing how sure I was with my reply, I realised that I had really recovered.

CHAPTER 8

MY UPHILL CLIMB

To find one's feet and get on the right path again after a many false detours takes time and commitment. I was now very determined to pick myself up and get on that right road. And I prayed that when I did I would never look back or get lost again.

I got a lot of professional help and I surrounded myself with just a few close friends. More than anything in the world I wanted things to be right and I would do anything in my power to be at peace with myself again. Physical illness is terrible, but when there is a war going on in one's mind it is almost impossible to see a light at the end of the tunnel. However, I believed that if I held on real tight to each minute of each hour of each day, week, month and year, I would get stronger and I would reach the light that would take me out of the darkness that had engulfed my very soul. I prayed to my dad and asked him to talk to God for me. In fact, I talked to every higher power I knew of to help me get my feet back on solid ground again.

I was drowning for such a long time and could not talk to anyone about it. I suppose I felt if I kept it to myself I could make it stop, but I couldn't. I recall one Christmas dinner when I had just beans on toast – on my own. I was so ashamed of being down so low I didn't want my family to see me like that as I knew I was quite an embarrassment to them. I wanted to get back up on my feet before I let them see me again. They never knew how down I really was. I still wished the phone would ring and someone would say Happy Christmas, but it never did ring. The loneliness continued and I sometimes wished I wouldn't make it until morning. I was drowning for such a long time and could not talk to anyone about it.

It was sometime later that Dr McInerney spoke to me about Aiséirí, an organisation that runs addiction treatment centres, and advised me to go to one. After some soul-searching, I agreed and went down to be assessed. Not to sound big-headed, but I thought everything was going to be done on my terms as I was a well-known public figure. I recall I didn't want to share a room, so I asked for a private room, and they told me that was no problem. I was given a date for admission. I got in touch with my band and, to save face, told them I was going to America for a while, and gave them holidays for a few weeks. I bought a few books, thinking I would catch up on a bit of reading while I was there, as I would have my own private room and that it would all be easy.

Little did I know what lay ahead. The Aiséirí experience was hard and it took a while for me to realise what the programme was about. We were free to leave if we wanted to and although I had not had a drink for months before going there, I knew when I had committed to this that I had to see it through. I met a great bunch of people there, but I remember one person leaving as he thought we were all crazy. I learnt a lot about myself. We had to talk openly about everything. Wednesday was family day, and my mother and brother John came down once to see me. Mam didn't like me being there. I think she felt it was an embarrassment to the family, and I can appreciate that. Also, I was the one she had depended on, and with me being in the limelight she felt I was degrading myself by being in such a place. But I was determined that this time I had to do this for me. I had to sort out my life and be happy with who I was.

I firmly believe today that I hadn't grown from the day I made that promise to Dad. Part of me hung onto that promise and I could not let it go. Yes, I felt sorry for myself at times as that was a huge burden to carry but, in fairness, I may have carried it to the extreme.

One day a counsellor brought up the relationship I had with my dad and how much I loved him, and one Friday she asked me to write a letter to my dad over the weekend. This was in the late

1980s and my dad had died in 1968. I was thinking, where will I post this letter, or how is it going to get to him? I thought the councillor was nuts. I looked at her and said, 'You've got to be kidding me.' 'No,' she said and told me to hand it in on Monday morning to the office. So I got my pen and paper and over the weekend I sat down and I wrote the letter as deeply as I felt, as truthfully as I knew how and on Monday morning I put it in the office. Nothing was said for a few days about my letter and then the bombshell dropped. I was told by Sister Eileen that the letter I had written was not love for my father. I was so insulted by her comment and felt so hurt that I turned my head away. Sister Eileen told me to look back at her and she continued by saying that, instead of love, this was a letter full of anger. I then realised that, yes, I was angry with my father for leaving me and for making me give that promise on his deathbed. Maybe it was irrational, but I was angry because my father left me; he was the person who should have been there to make decisions for my family, not me. As it was group therapy, everybody heard what was being said, but I didn't mind. At last things were finally being put into place for me.

On Sundays people walked to the local church to Mass, but I was advised not to go because I might be recognised. Indeed, I remember one Sunday newspaper reporter came to the gates of Aiséirí to ask about me being in there, but Aiséirí protected me totally. No one would ever know that I was there unless I revealed it later.

It took a while for me to come to terms with this new way of life as I had to make a lot of changes. I owe so much to Sister Eileen and the staff in Aiséirí and to Dr McInerney, all of whom believed in me. I slowly began to have that belief in myself; but I knew I was fragile so I was really careful. 'One day at a time' was the advice, and how true that was.

The industry I was involved in was a paradise for an alcoholic. Maybe that's another reason I'm at peace now as I am not involved much anymore. I knew I had reached rock bottom – I was down so far the only way for me was up, as the saying goes. I was once told by a great friend: 'Margaret, when you get yourself right, everything else will fall into place and will be right with you.' And it turned out to be true.

Little by little I started on my journey back. I took small steps, steps that suited me. Yes, there were people who would offer me drink, but for the most part they didn't know and didn't mean any harm and that didn't bother me. However, one night a person whom I thought was a friend 'spiked' my drink with alcohol while I was out of the room, but on returning I saw it being done. I never touched the drink, but I knew I would never again call that person 'friend'. I would never, ever want that kind of life again.

My confidence was growing. I regained my self-pride, and what I had struggled with in the past became easier for me to deal with. I know a lot of beautiful people who have had a drink problem and they are special. Today I know I am special.

I am not going to say that I didn't slip up during that period and that it was easy, because it wasn't. Some of the things I did at that time I am not proud of. I'm happy now to be able to talk about those experiences quite openly. That took some time for me to do. Little by little the steps I took were getting longer and every time I stood up I stood a little longer and taller. I can be in company now with people who are taking a drink and it doesn't bother me. Alcohol and I were never good friends.

I was to sing one night in London, and as I walked in the door I heard a voice call, 'Margo! Margo!' I looked over and saw a homeless man sitting on the ground. He said he just wanted to hear me sing, but would not be allowed in. I asked him to wait. I went and found the person in charge and I pleaded with him to let the man in and that I would take responsibility for him. There was a little balcony in the hall and I put him there. Before I left London I made sure he was okay, and we stayed in touch. This man wanted to get sober, and I helped as much as I could and he did finally get there. Sadly, when he got sober he became ill and was given about six months to live. I am proud to say he died sober, as was his wish. I was there when he was laid to rest and I knew he died happy. He too was a very special person. No hill is too hard to climb if we really want to badly enough.

I genuinely believe that I didn't suffer from depression, but there was a darkness, call it by whatever label you wish, that would engulf me for long periods. I was not in control of the life I was in and I should have been. I take the blame for allowing people to use and abuse me, but didn't have the nerve or strength to stand up to these people, afraid that I would lose my job and that my mam and family would suffer as well as myself. I know today that no one could sell what Margo had in her voice except Margo, but I was not able to stand up to those in the music business who did not give one thought for me as a person and what I was going through.

The road back was hard and long but it was worth every single step. I got my confidence back slowly and my life was to change again, this time for the better.

CHAPTER 9

A SIGN FROM A
HIGHER POWER

In 1992, County Donegal was in the All-Ireland Final for the very first time. I had a big hit with a tribute song, 'Walking Tall in Donegal'. It was a great song, written by Castleblayney songwriter Henry McMahon, with Kevin McCooey, who was my manager at that time. Kevin has a great knowledge of Gaelic football, whereas Henry admitted to me that he has not. All in all, though, I believe it is one of Henry's best compositions and I sang it with great pride. That year was so special in Donegal and I was so much a part of it with the song. I was on my way to sing at a victory dance in Donegal town when, just five or six miles from Castleblayney, a car crossed the road in front of me. The driver was elderly and had drink taken. As I swerved to try and avoid impact I crashed into a brick wall. My friend Shirley Jones was in the car with me and suffered cracked ribs and neck injuries, and I too had neck injuries, as well as a cracked sternum. We were taken to hospital, so I never got to Donegal for the victory dance, after all. I was very sore in my right breast for a long time afterwards and I am convinced it contributed to what was to follow. In 1993 I found a lump in my breast which resulted in me having a lumpectomy. I was so scared of the unknown, but I had the surgery in Dublin's Mater Hospital and the end result was good.

I went back singing right away, but I was only a few days back when I began to feel ill and my wound was extremely sore. I had developed septicaemia. It took me some time to recover from that. In fact, I understood from the medical profession that I was lucky to survive it at all. Thanks to Dr Flanagan, I made a full recovery.

At the beginning of 1996 I started to feel very tired; some days I didn't feel like I could get out of bed and that was not the norm for me. I continued to work at both dances and concerts but a little voice inside me was telling me all wasn't right. I went to the doctor and had tests done, but everything seemed okay.

In November 1996 I went on a tour of Australia and while I was there I knew something was terribly wrong. I was sleeping all the time in between the shows. I managed to complete the tour and boarded the plane in Melbourne for home. I was exhausted. I went to my doctor and discovered that while I was away she had found that the platelets in my blood were very low. It needed investigation.

Although I had never felt so exhausted, I decided that I would honour whatever work had already been booked. I recall it was around Christmastime and I had work backed up quite tightly. I was singing in the hotel in Glencolmcille on a Friday night and on the Saturday I was booked in for Logues in Cranford. After the dance on Friday night I felt awful. I tried to get to the bathroom in the morning but found it difficult to walk and my breathing was also affected. A lady I knew from home had the contact number for Fr Des Sweeney, who has the wonderful gift of healing; she made an appointment for me to see him. Fr Des lived in Ramelton, which was on my way to the venue on Saturday night. I got an appointment with him before the show. My booking agent and a friend were travelling with me, and at that stage I could not walk unaided from the car. They both helped me in. I sat beside Fr Des as he prayed over me. I would have done anything or gone anywhere to feel better, but divine intervention guided me to Ramelton and to Fr Des. I remember saying to him, 'I don't think I'll be able to sing tonight,' and he replied, 'You will sing like a lark.' Before I left him I said, 'I feel so weak that I don't think I will see you again, Father'. He looked at me and replied, 'Don't worry, you'll visit me many times.' I walked back to the car unaided, and I sang that night without a problem.

On 20 December 1996 I was diagnosed with a blood disorder called Dyscrasia and I underwent many, many tests over the Christmas of 1996. On 6 January 1997 I went to the Charlemont Clinic in Dublin and underwent more tests. A week later I was admitted to St James's Hospital and because of underlying problems with my blood I was advised in January by my specialist that my life of touring on the road was over – and, to be honest, my body agreed. I was totally burnt out. I knew I would never be involved in music in the same way again. I took the advice of my specialist because I knew he was right. I knew I would greatly miss the singing and meeting people. I was aware that I would never be involved in the music business in quite the same way again. But I felt God above was guiding me through this. Still, to this day I really miss what I had done all my life, even back to when I was a little girl.

As usual, lots of different stories were going around about what was wrong with me, but the outpouring of love and prayers that I received from my fans and friends all over the globe was just unbelievable. I will never forget how cared for and loved I felt.

Day by day I began to get stronger and stronger and then one evening as I was sitting in my home in Castleblayney the phone rang. It was the 'healing nun', Sr Briege McKenna. Although she is Irish, she lives in Tampa, Florida. She spoke with me and told me she was on her way to Fatima to the shrine of our Blessed Lady; she had heard I was ill when she touched down in Dublin. We arranged to meet in All Hallows College in Dublin. I had felt a great improvement since I met with Fr Des Sweeney and I told this to Sr Briege. With a faraway look in her eye she said, 'Yes, you do, and now I will ask God to help you more.' I sometimes felt it difficult to feel my legs and the tiredness I experienced was unreal, but in the days that followed our meeting I began to get stronger. I dared not even try to explain what was happening inside of me, but I knew it was a healing process. I always remember my late father talking one time to me about religion. He said, 'We are Catholics and we are Christians, but we must respect every person we meet. They may not be of our faith but they are as good as and sometimes better than we are.' I never forgot those words. I know I'm not perfect but I know that Fr Des Sweeney and Sr Briege McKenna have a power greater than me, and I believe I was touched by God and the Blessed Lady. I have no doubt in my mind that while I was in their company I received great healing through the power of prayer.

Although I could never go back touring the way that I used to, through these two servants of God I was given the knowledge that I must stop what I was doing and take stock of what lay ahead. I still didn't seem to be able to pray and when I said that to Fr Brian Darcy he told me to let other people pray for me, so that's what I did. I handed it over, and then each day I would simply talk to God and to my father. It is a slow process and as I write I still have a way to go. I have to keep it simple and I am a worrier by nature, so sometimes I find keeping it simple is pretty difficult!

I know I panicked when my dad passed away and I worried so much about my capabilities in taking care of my mam and the family. 'Care' is perhaps the wrong word because that was my mother's job, but I had to provide financially to keep the wheels turning. I always thought of myself as an under-achiever and honestly didn't give either Margaret the person, or Margo the singer the credit each of them was due, which is something I should not have allowed to happen. I would allow people to talk down to me, but that is in the past now. I now no longer had to worry about looking after my family, all of them were able to provide for themselves now, my Mam too. When Dad was gone I was proud to be in a position to help Mam and if I never made a promise to my father I would still be proud to do as I did.

I attended hospital in Dublin for a number of years after that and one day I had a long talk with my specialist. I suggested to him that maybe I could do a small few 'Margo' shows and meet up with my numerous fans and friends. He agreed, but he told me that my body would dictate how much I could do. I tested this out in two places, Castlebar, County Mayo, and Killarney, County Kerry. I didn't do the two shows back-to-back, but took a rest in between. It worked a treat, so afterwards, with my musical director Clive Culbertson on board, I was able to enjoy these little shows. The crowds were as big as ever and I really loved being able to do what came naturally to me. I was grateful to God for giving me the strength to do that and it was enough. I felt involved again. I'd only stopped touring because I had to; I don't believe I would be here today if I had continued. Although I wasn't physically strong enough to continue fulltime in show business, I will be eternally grateful for the wonderful relationship I still have with my audience.

When I sing now I am not in show business. I feel it's a little piece of me I give to the people who love and enjoy Margo and in return the audience give back to me everything I could ask for: their love. Today I take care of myself and have good friends all around me, but above all I'm happy within myself. I'm not rich financially, but I'm rich in other ways and I don't have an expensive lifestyle. I enjoy doing the simple things in life. If you ask me today to list the most important things that happened in the past ten years I would say meeting Fr Sweeney and Sr Briege, as well as my devotion to Padre Pio, along with all the prayers from people who let me know I was special to them. This really touched me. I have no doubt that it helped me. To put it in other words, a Higher Power took me by the hand.

CHAPTER 10

MY TRUE SELF

With all of the things that had happened to me through-out my life, I can honestly say my self-worth was almost gone. When I became ill and stopped touring I decided I would go about finding out what happened to my recordings. I will not bore you with all of the details, but it was very messy. I discovered that in 1977 my then manager John McNally sold all of my recordings to Outlet Records in Belfast for £37,500; the exchange was made from the boot of one car to another in Belfast and the transaction was never discussed with me. I would hear about a new cassette, LP or CD of mine being released; I would go to the record stores and buy it so that I could hear it. Some of the recordings were not mastered, some just had guide voices on them, that is, they were not even finished properly. On several occasions I requested a meeting with the Belfast company, but they would never agree to it. When I phoned, no one was willing to speak to me. To this day I do not know what Billy McBurney, who owned Outlet Records then, looks like.

I decided that it was worth fighting for my rights. I was the first female artist in Ireland to take court action of this kind against a record company. In December 2002, I sat in a courtroom in Belfast to hear that all of the recordings – vinyl, CD and cassette – and all works of 'Margo O'Donnell' belonged to me and me alone. I have all the court documents to prove my case; I won my case and received a reasonable settlement. When my records were selling in their thousands I lost out on all of the huge money that was made. No one even said sorry.

I was right to fight to claim what was mine. My master tapes are now back where they belong, with me, and no one will ever take my recordings from me again. Naturally, I am sad that I did not receive the financial gain that was due to me and now I will never know how rich I could have been! But I guess I have to live with that. No good would come of constantly looking back and thinking of 'what might have been' and how much I was wronged by people who I thought were, and should have been, on my side.

Someone in the music business who supported me through the trauma of my court case and who has never shown anything but loyalty and care for me is Shay Hennessy. Shay and I have known each other for over thirty years. As a young man he travelled the country with my albums and single chart records. He went from distribution to having his own record label, and through all the years our paths were always crossing. He was a great fan of Margo's and is now the main man in charge of my recordings. When I started my case against Billy McBurney and Outlet, Shay had already been involved in two other cases, one concerning Horslips and the other concerning the Dubliners. His knowledge was priceless to all of us. Shay was with me in the Nuremore Hotel in Carrickmacross on the day we settled our business with Outlet Records. I was so happy that Shay came on board with me and I have say thank you to him for helping me to realise my true self-worth; I will always be grateful to Shay and he will always be a big part of my life.

When my court case ended, the reality of the fact that my recordings belonged to me was really only dawning on me. I asked Shay to get all the original master tapes so I could bring them home; all I wanted was to have them with me. When I got them home I sat there for days and just kept looking at them. When it finally sank in that they were mine I knew I was looking at what should have made me a very rich woman. I gathered up the tapes and gave them back to Shay to be sorted and re-mastered. I felt I had to try and salvage something out of the injustice that had been done to me. As I write, all of my old recordings have been re-mastered and nearly all have been re-issued on compilation CDs and they are all available – and, more important, these CDs have my stamp of approval on each one of them.

I can honestly say getting to know myself again and, more importantly, getting to know the real me has brought a great sense of peace to my inner self. I like to have nice things in life just as much as anyone, but I don't have a very expensive lifestyle. I like simple things and I keep life as simple as possible. I know today who my friends are but I am still learning more each and every day. However, today I know what I have and I cannot waste time dwelling on what should have been. I refuse to let the past destroy what I have. I succeeded in getting my recordings back and I also have my life back on track and I intend to live it simply and the best way I can.

It amuses me now to remember how, down through the years, I would meet people who would say: Margo, you must be worth a fortune. My response was always the same: Oh! I can't even spend the interest on my savings! I don't think that my family were even aware of how much money I lost. I hid all the pain I was going through and thought I could weather the rough times alone, but now I know that is not possible.

Believe me, in my career I met some of the greatest crooks – as well as some of the best people – in the music business; and, indeed, sometimes I felt like a magnet, attracting negative things towards me. Maybe part of it was the fact that the business was almost totally controlled by men, and even now I see instances where women are not treated equally in this sort of situation. My strongest advice to any artist would be: control your own recordings at all times and make sure you select very carefully those in whom you put your trust. If my unpleasant experience with some of the people I encountered in the music business helps one person to avoid a similar situation I will be happy. When I learnt what my earnings from my recordings could have been, I felt sick for what was done to me. But at that stage I was strong enough to cope with it without resorting to the demon drink. It's highly unlikely that I'll get back the earnings that I was cheated out of. I will never have millions in the bank, or huge mansions to live in, it doesn't take millions or mansions to make someone like me happy. I feel blessed with the love of friends and my wonderful fans, along with the contentment I can now enjoy.

After my experiences in show business you can imagine how I felt when my youngest brother, Daniel, announced to me that he wanted to sing. I was deeply concerned for his welfare and for his future. I did try to tell him that the road he had chosen could be a difficult and cruel one, but thankfully Daniel was lucky with those he had around him and has succeeded beyond our wildest dreams.

In all of the things that happened to me I want to say that I'm not without blame. I trusted people too easily. I was young and inexperienced and had been raised with people for whom honesty was second nature, so I guess I wasn't prepared for the ruthlessness of some in show business for whom the bottom line is always money, not the artist who is making it for them. Even though I wasn't fortunate enough to have a college education, I was blessed with a lot of common sense, but I should have been more alert to what was going on. My vision was clouded or maybe I just couldn't face what I really knew was wrong. I have never in my life knowingly done any great wrong to anyone. Perhaps when I took a drink my judgement may not have been a hundred percent, and for anything I may have done to hurt anyone during that period I am truly sorry.

My life plan did not go as I had hoped and dreamed it would. When I joined the Keynotes at thirteen years of age I did it as a thing I loved, but only planned to do it for a short time while still at school. It was a hobby to me, and I loved it, but as a career – no, I was going to be a nurse. That was my plan, for sure. But at thirteen I was able to pay for all my school needs and give some money to my Mam as well. Ten shillings a night back in 1964 was *money*! Even when we recorded our first record in 1968 I was still certain of a nursing career. However, when my dad died all that changed.

I realise now how serious a commitment it was, but my family needed looking out for and I felt it was my duty to do so. Daniel was just six years old. John was nearly two years older than me but after Dad passed away John got ill, and I replaced him to take care of my clan. Later on, when I left the Keynotes, I brought John on the road with me and he had the job of driving me to all my shows. I was the only one in my family at that time who was in a position to take care of things. Sometimes I would worry about how I could carry out my responsibility and that put a lot of pressure on me.

As I come to my fiftieth anniversary in show business, and despite all the trauma, recalling the memories of the great success I have had is quite a pleasure. I can recall halls and other venues I performed in where the 'Full House' signs were a regular feature. There could be two or three thousand people inside dancing to our music, and that is a great memory.

I can honestly say that Margo has stood the test of time. Margo, the singer or entertainer or whatever people wish to call me, is still in big demand to this very day and that, I think, says it all. My ever-loyal fans and friends keep me going and I'm always so very grateful. Margaret O'Donnell, the Kincasslagh lass born on 6 February 1951, is doing okay; she is rich with friendship and loves the simple life.

If I were to join Margo and Margaret together I would find that each is so proud of the other.

Throughout my life I felt that as long as I was useful I was wanted, but today I look in the mirror and I know I am important to me. I feel a real person is looking back at me, someone who has known success and failure, was happy and sad, experienced good and bad. I can still get hurt. I haven't stopped feeling, but I feel proud of my true self and I look at myself in the mirror and whisper: I have given and shared everything I have. So, Margaret and Margo: 'Well done.'

CHAPTER 11

PEOPLE I HAVE MET

AND MY FANS

There is a saying: 'never forget the old for the new' and I have never forgotten the friends I made as I was growing up. They are extra special.

If I had a hundred years more to live, I could never explain how much all my fans mean to me, and believe me I do not say that lightly. I have met some great people and made wonderful friends on my life's journey.

When I began touring I met new friends just like everybody does. When I performed in Dublin ballrooms there were lots of country people working and living there. We would get talking and discover lots of things in common, apart from the music we loved. At that stage the fans and I were from the same age group. On many occasions I would end up back at their place having a cup of tea and chatting like old friends. The North Circular Road was a place where I often visited my fans and although the years have passed we still keep in contact; most of them are now married and have their families reared, but they still come to my shows.

In the 1970s I got to know almost all of the people in the music business here in Ireland. This small country of ours is filled with talent and we have produced great singers, songwriters and musicians down through the years.

The Country Music Festival in Wembley, London, was like no other, all of the American Country legends appeared there. I was so lucky to share the stage with all the great Country singers from Nashville, Tennessee: Johnny Cash, Loretta Lynn, Conway Twitty, Dottie West, Lynn Anderson, Tammy Wynette, Glen Campbell, The Statler Brothers, George Jones, to name but a few, as well as my favourite, Kitty Wells, 'The Queen of Country Music'. I also toured with Hank Locklin and Red Sovine in England and with Slim Whitman here in Ireland. I feel so, so lucky to have walked and talked with these great icons of Country music.

One time in Nashville I went out to Madison to visit Kitty Wells. I stood outside, looking at her tour bus – I wanted a photo of myself standing beside it. Kitty saw me and said, 'I see you were checking out my bus'. She went on, 'There's a difference between that bus and the ones the new stars have today. Do you know what the difference is?' When I said no, she smiled and said, 'My bus is paid for.' Kitty Wells had a little museum in Madison; I visited there one day, many years after I had met Kitty in Wembley. I went in the door and, leaning by a chair at the entrance, sat a full life-size cut-out of Kitty Wells. As I was going through the museum I came across another life-size cut-out of Kitty – until it moved and touched my hand! I almost fainted. Kitty and I laughed so much about that, and she went on to give me a personal tour of the museum. What a privilege. I performed at Wembley with Kitty and I took my brother Daniel to meet her there – I can still recall the expression on Daniel's face when he came face to face with her.

Someone else with whom I stayed in touch was Jean Sheppard. Jean was first married to Hawshaw Hawkins who was killed in the 1963 plane crash with Patsy Cline and Cowboy Copas. Another great friend of mine was the unforgettable Skeeter Davis; I sang with her and Jeannie Pruett and Jan Howard on the Grand Ole Opry in Nashville, a memory that is very special.

Skeeter Davis became a real friend and I miss her. I kept in touch up until her demise some years ago. Skeeter's real name was Mary Frances Penick, and she was born in Glencoe, Kentucky. She had a singing partner called Betty Jack Davis and their first big hit record as The Davis Sisters in 1953 (two years after I was born) was 'I Forgot More Than You'll Ever Know' that went right to the top of the charts. They sounded wonderful together, with the special harmony they made. Skeeter Davis on her own will be remembered for her No.1 hit 'The End of the World', that crossed over to the pop charts. I meet younger people today who know that song because DJs still play it. I have many memories of Skeeter, all wonderful. I remember we sat on Jeanne Pruett's front porch one day and recalled songs we knew and loved. Jeanne Pruett had a big hit with 'Satin Sheets', and both she and Skeeter were part of the The Grand Ladies of the Opry, a great honour.

I was there on the last night that Tammy Wynette performed at the Opry. Jan Howard and I went to see her when she came off stage and she was so ill. Jan and I cried that night, as did a lot of folk at the show. I guess we all knew it was Tammy's last performance. All the people I have met in Nashville have been wonderful: Waylon Jennings, Willie Nelson, Kris Kristofferson, Minnie Pearl, Bill Anderson, Jimmy Dickens, Lorrie Morgan, Marty Stuart, and one of my great favourites, Connie Smith. Porter Wagoner gave Philomena Begley and myself our first spot together on the Opry when we went with the late Tony Lough-man to record our duet album in Nashville.

Dottie West was a lady I first met at the Country Festival in Wembley, London. Dottie was such a classy singer and I was in awe of her wonderful voice. She was killed in a road accident not far from the Opry, another great loss to Country music.

Jan Howard is another Grand Lady of the Opry and is always kind to me when I visit Nashville. I would never have believed, way back in 1964 when I sang as a hobby with the Keynotes, that I would meet all these wonderful people and great legends of Country music, and that I would write about them, but I really did get these special gifts of knowing these great people and I thank God for all the blessings I got from having my life touched by them.

I also have the most wonderful admiration for a lady who works endlessly behind the scenes in the music business. Her name is Phyllis Hill and I met her through Skeeter Davis when Phyllis worked with TNN Television, a Nashville network. She is now involved in publishing. We've had great times together and we always stay in touch.

Kim Vance, who now lives in Branson, Missouri, has always a place in my heart. There are hundreds more that I could mention, from Grandpa Jones to Vince Gill, Ricky Skaggs and the great Stonewall Jackson … the list could go on and on.

I was privileged to meet Liz and Casey Anderson, the parents of Lynn Anderson, who had a mega-hit with 'I Never Promised You a Rose Garden'. Liz and Casey have written some of the greatest Country songs of our lifetime that have been covered by artists such as Brenda Lee, Merle Haggard, Del Reeves and Conway Twitty. One night, before I was about to leave for Nashville, I answered my phone and on the other end was Liz. She had got my number from my friend Bobby O'Brien and she knew I had recorded many of her songs. Bobby was from New York State and had loved my singing since he was twelve years old!

I had no greater fan. He made contact with Liz and put her in touch with me. He loved the songs Liz had written over the years almost as much as I did. I was thrilled that Bobby had hooked me up with Liz.

I really connected with Liz and Casey. On the day we met, I waited for them in the Hall of Fame Hotel, just down from Music Row in Nashville. As soon as they appeared I just had this feeling of warmth and ease. We spent as much time as possible sharing songs and exchanging stories. Liz was a straight talker, which suited me fine as I'm a straight talker too. Liz, Casey and I loved one another unconditionally. We would sit on her little front porch and she would let me hear new songs that maybe I could record and, believe me, if I sang one note wrong Liz would stop playing and let me know she was not impressed. I miss her so much. I wrote a tribute song with Joe McShane, simply called 'Liz Anderson', which will be on my CD box set for my 50th Anniversary; the CD with this song will be 'Songs by the Fireside'. The box set will be released to coincide with my book. I still keep in close touch with Casey.

Tribute to Liz Anderson

In the year of '27, in the State of Minnesota
The month of January, in the heart of the cold winter
That's where a great songwriter first opened her eyes
I'm sure the howlin' wind that night sang a lullaby

When I was just a young girl, I joined the music scene
I'd pick out all the sweetest songs and words I'd like to sing
I didn't know who wrote my favourite music way back then
But that writer was my hero, who became my dearest friend

A master with her pen in hand, guitar upon her knee
Many times out on her front porch she'd spend some time
　　with me
She made me feel so special but that always was her way
With her heart of gold Liz Anderson lives with me every day

She told me how she wrote Merle Haggard's 'Fugitive' one day
She wrote it with her husband, while driving down the highway
She said we've missed the turn, now that's an awful pity
Then Casey said, down every road, there's always another city

A master with her pen in hand, guitar upon her knee
Many times out on her front porch she'd spend some time
　　with me
She made me feel so special but that always was her way
With her heart of gold Liz Anderson lives with me every day

Sometimes the brightest star you know will sit back in the shade
So pure, kind and truthful, a gift that's heaven made
I know we'll meet again some day, when life is evermore
Tonight you're in God's loving arms, upon that golden shore

Yes, the year was '27, in the State of Minnesota
The month of January, in the heart of the cold winter
That's where a great songwriter first opened her eyes
I'm sure the howlin' wind that night sang a lullaby

Till we meet again, my dear friend, Liz Anderson, Goodbye.

In time I met another great lady from the Smokey Mountains –
the one and only Dolly Parton. Again my friend Bobby O'Brien
was involved. The first time he and I and my friend Shirley Jones
visited Pigeon Forge in east Tennessee, Dolly and I had never
met. I had been in touch with Louis Owens, Dolly's uncle on her
mother's side. Louis and Uncle Bill Owens and Dolly's cousins
all performed at Dollywood Theme Park so I would go up and
sing with them. One evening after the park closed we went up
to where Dolly was born. Dolly bought all of the land where her
dad, Lee, was a sharecropper and where they were all born and
raised. Bobby, Shirley and I drove way up into the mountains and
found the nearest place to heaven I have ever seen. I could see the
stream and flowers Dolly wrote about in 'God's Colouring Book',
a song that Dolly and I went on to record later on. If you can
imagine the wooden forts that surrounded the army in the old
cowboy movies, Dolly had that kind of surround, with security
all around. We could see a light flickering in the window of the
house in the trees and there was a dog running around. I wanted
to get a message to Dolly if she was there. I called 'here boy' to

This is me with my brother Daniel. He started his career on stage with me and has gone on to be a wonderful star, known all over the world.

The two 'Girls from Donegal'! I'm here with the original, Bridie Gallagher.

Here I am performing with Brendan Shine at a tribute concert for Brendan.

Prince Charles with the Queen
– of Country and Irish!

Gay Byrne has been a fan – and I
was on his 'Late Late Show' way
back in 1969.

I like to travel – in
all different ways!
Here I am, ready
for the road.

This is me performing at the Grand Ole Opry in Tennessee, the mecca for Country Music fans. What an honour!

With the greatest of them all – our beloved Dolly.

I really admired Dottie West, and am lucky to have met her.

Here I am with Loretta Lynn (left) and my friend Shirley Jones

This picture was taken at Tammy Wynette's last show at the Grand Ole Opry in Nashville.

Two of my best friends in the business, Skeeter Davis and Liz Anderson. Here we are recording at a studio in Nashville.

Still performing, doing the thing I love best. This is me on stage after fifty years in the music business.

This is me with Joe McShane in Chicago.

It was a great honour on my fiftieth anniversary in show business to be invited to sing for our president, Michael D Higgins.

Here I am with two of my favourite Castleblayney men, Paddy Cole and one of my favourite Irish singers, Big Tom.

I also performed with the wonderful Ricky Skaggs at the Grand Ole Opry.

Here I am with Porter Wagoner at the Grand Ole Opry.

A fine group indeed! I am standing behind Philomena Begley in this photo, taken with the Grand Ladies of Opry at a filming session in Nashville.

I was delighted to work with the great Charley Pride.

In Nashville again, this time with Crystal Gayle, a wonderful lady.

This 'Donegal Person of the Year' award was so precious as it was from my home county. Here I am with Pat the Cope Gallagher, Shiela McGinley and Martin McGettigan.

MARGO

A special celebration and performance after thirty-five years on stage – and now I've reached fifty!

A wonderful man and a great performer – here I am with Declan Nerney.

With Mam, how sad to have lost her this year. We'll all miss her very much.

the dog and he came running. Bobby took the inlay paper from one of my tapes and I wrote a note saying, *Hi Dolly, this is Margo from Ireland. I'm a singer and would love to see you and have a chat.* I signed my name and rolled the paper around the dog's collar and tried to chase him home, but no matter how I tried he wouldn't leave me and go back to the house. Later that night I went to Dolly's sister Stella's place. I had appeared with Stella in Wembley and she had a place called 'Stella's Hat House' where new talent would sing every night. I met Stella and we spent some time together. I told her about the message I'd put in the dog's collar and she laughed so much. She told me Dolly was in Los Angeles and their brother Bobby was house sitting. Next day I sang with Dolly's folks again at Dollywood and we then went out to visit her parents. Stella must have told them I might be calling. When I got out of the car at the gate Lee called out to come on up. We sat on the front porch and talked for quite a while. Every time I went back to east Tennessee afterwards I would always visit. When I came back to Ireland I was diagnosed with my blood disorder and I had to curtail my work and touring. Through all of this Louis Owens continued to send me tracks to add my voice to, which I did. The tracks were then sent back to Louis and although I felt I could not go to Nashville and record with Dolly's family, my friend Bobby thought it would lift my spirits and so it was arranged. I flew once again to Nashville, met Louis and his son Ritchie Owens, who to this day tours with Dolly in her band. Ritchie had the studio at his house, so we set to work – Dolly's cousins, Uncle Bill, Uncle Louis and Aunt Dorothy Jo all arrived and we worked day after day and into the night and set down the foundation for my CD titled 'The Highway of My Life'.

It was the greatest experience of my life. Then came the day when Dolly came to town and to the studio; even her relations were on a high. She was a vision in blue as she got off her bus. Right away we hit it off. Hope Powell, a famous photographer of Country singers, was on hand to do our photo shoot and I felt so loved by everyone. Dolly Parton and her family certainly pushed the boat out for Margo O'Donnell – and it didn't stop there, other recordings took place and more photo shoots. Dolly told me once, 'Believe in yourself.' She said I was 'one of the best' and that I was special to her. Dolly has written a little bit for this book. Dolly and her family stepped up to the mark for me and I will never forget that, never.

On a different note, the year I toured Australia I finished in Sydney but then I went back to Melbourne to spend some time with friends. I stayed in the Hyatt Hotel in the city, and guess who was staying two floors above me, none other than Michael Jackson. It was something to watch all the Jackson fans; the hysteria was mind-blowing. I did get to meet him and I had a photo taken with him, and he knew I was an Irish singer. He made time for all the fans and I think of him very positively. Who are we to judge him? We haven't walked in Michael Jackson's shoes. He was a wonderful entertainer and I am so honoured to have met him.

CHAPTER 12

THE CHARITIES I AM
DEDICATED TO

It is always good to be able to give something back, and, whenever I could throughout my career, I was happy to give my time and talent in support of charitable causes I believed in. I would always remember one important thing – it was God who gave me my gift of singing so I was always ready to use that gift in the service of others. Way back in the 1970s I got involved in the building of a church in South Africa where a priest from near my home, Fr Anthony O'Donnell (no relation) was serving in missionary work. He would keep me up to date with progress on the project. He has been retired for a long time now but I hope that the church is still serving its great purpose.

Then there were the many fishing tragedies around our coastline which had a particular pull on my heartstrings as a lot of my mother's family and my cousins are involved in fishing. Close friends of mine have lost loved ones over the years and it was a privilege to give my voice and my time to help in bringing them some financial security.

In 2006-2007 I was elected Donegal Person of the Year, a great honour. In my acceptance speech I said jokingly that it was long overdue, but, looking back, perhaps it came at just the right time. For the following twelve months I donated my time to all the requests I could possibly fit in. It was really hard work but it was worth every minute, knowing that I had given that year to the charities.

About six years ago I was contacted by Michael Boyle, a man from Aranmore Island just off the Donegal coast but who has lived his life in Chicago. He asked if I would come over to do a concert there. The proceeds were going to charities headed by the St Patrick Fathers, whose head office is in Chicago. I explained that I'd had to stop touring because of my illness and that I didn't have a band anymore. But Michael was very persistent. He said to me, 'People love Margo so much over here; all you have to do is come and stand on the stage!' I thought about it some more and I got a load of my backing music ready and let him hear it. I said, 'If you think this will work, I will come and sing with these tracks and put on a concert.' Now, it's pretty hard to perform to backing tracks – you've got to be alert and not miss a beat – if you have a band they can slow down or speed up, whatever the case may be, but with the backing tracks you are on your own. Michael insisted it would be great, and so it was.

That was six years ago and every year I do a charity concert there, and it's always a sell-out. Mike's wife, Cathy, and all of the crew treat me like family. The people involved work really hard, with Fr Karl as the head man. My friend Johnny Gleeson gives his services and my song-writing partner, Joe McShane, is close at hand at all times. I get to see Fr Peter Rookey, this wonderful healing priest who is very special. Mike and Nancy Kenny and their family have been friends for many years so it's like going home. Although Mike has since passed away, I always spend some time with his wife, Nancy, and her family when I'm in Chicago.

A couple of years ago I was honoured by the Donegal Association in New York as New York's Donegal Person of the year, 2011. The commemorative plaque has the words: 'In grateful recognition and in sincere appreciation of your distinguished career and your contribution to the World of Music, The people of Donegal in the city of New York pay tribute to you this evening as a loyal and dedicated person who has earned the respect and admiration of New York's Irish American Community.' The award was presented on Saturday, 19 March, and was signed by Katie Barratt, President, and Rosina Gallagher, Chairperson of the Donegal Association of New York City.

To me this was such a special night and I really enjoyed every minute. Two days before, on St Patrick's Day, I led the Donegal Association group in the parade down 5th Avenue in New York City. You could never imagine how proud I was on that day. Awards and recognition are wonderful, but to be hailed by one's own people brings it all to an extra high level. It meant a lot to be chosen here in Ireland as Donegal Person of 2006, but New York was a wonderful and magical surprise, the icing on the cake!

In terms of my charitable work, I like to know who I'm helping and I am happy that with all the charities I have worked for the money raised goes right to the cause, which is very important. When I read now of the little street kids in Brazil, or an orphanage in Haiti, or the 'Water for Life' programme in Africa, I know I have helped donate towards a better life for these people who live in our world but have so little of its riches.

Back home, I enjoy doing the yearly concert for the Mullaghduff Band. My father played in the senior Mullaghduff Band, as did my brother John, while Daniel carried the flag. The concert helps to fill the kitty and keep the band going.

I'm involved with various charities for the mentally handicapped because of my nephew and godchild, Joey, who has a lot of special needs. There is a beautiful day centre in Dungloe, County Donegal, where Joey goes each day and where all of the carers are wonderful. You have to be a really special person to do that work and every time I go there to visit I feel so much love around me.

As I stood in my garden at my home in County Monaghan one day I thought of Joey. I closed my eyes and I captured his face in my mind. When I opened my eyes again I saw a rainbow – all the beautiful colours almost dazzled me, and through them somehow I could see Joey with his wonderful face and smile, and when I reached out to touch him I almost touched a rainbow, and that is how this song came to be.

I Almost Touched a Rainbow

God sent us down an angel and it really changed our lives
A smiley face of wisdom, a cheeky look in those blue eyes
A child sent down from heaven, a sweetheart young and true
No need to chase the rainbows, they all come to visit you

I often prayed to my dear Lord that you lived in my world
To know how much I love you as my tears they drop like pearls
Then a big smile opens up the night just like the silvery moon
Your eyes begin to sparkle and you light up every room

As I reach out I almost touched a rainbow
But I guess that heaven only knows
If a message from my heart can truly be
A sign you can feel it knowingly
This love I have inside for you, my Joey

They say there is a reason for all within God's plan
We sometimes shouldn't question what we don't understand
A smile, a clear blue sky, at play in dreamy games
As I watch you sleep I realise our paths are just the same.

Thank you, Joey, for all you have given me. I am so honoured to have you in my life. I hope to be able to continue to perform charity concerts for many years to come.

CHAPTER 13

CONTENTMENT IN

MY LIFE

No one knows what lies ahead of them and I could never have imagined that my life would have so many interesting turns and twists. Donegal, my native county, is the most wonderful place in the world; it is a place to which I will always be connected and I will always have a strong bond with all of my neighbours and friends who still live there.

In 1996 I went back home to film a video. All my neighbours took part and I didn't need to ask them twice, they all did everything I asked of them and more. Eileen Oglesby (now Mrs

McPhillips) from Owey Island, gave me her fishing boat and her crew and helped me to round up everything I needed for all the effects. Mary McGarvey, another friend, made her thatched cottages available to me. I will always be grateful for the support and neighbourliness of these people who were unstinting in their love and respect for me. All the success and achievements I have had in my life would mean nothing if I didn't remember where and when it all began, how I have arrived in this special place in my mind and, indeed, in my life right now.

Has life changed me in fifty years in the business? If it hadn't, I would worry. Life had changed for me and through all the years so many things changed the course of my destiny. I know I too have changed, but I still have the same heart as when I came away from home all those years ago as my career took off. My life from then on was always away from my family in Donegal. I do wish I was with family more, but we are all busy doing our own thing in life and I feel sad about that.

All the highs and the lows, hitting rock bottom, getting back up and starting all over again; reaching out for help and getting it; then taking another a wrong turn and going back down that dark road, but always getting back up, until one day I reached the special dawn of a New Beginning and finally finding me, Margaret and Margo, totally respectful of each other. Today I try never to let anyone or anything lead me down anywhere I don't think is right for me.

Nowadays I live just on the edge of the town of Castleblayney,

County Monaghan. I moved here in 1992. My then manager Kevin McCooey and my band were based here so it was the right place to be. Contentment, I think, has arrived. I have a nice, comfortable home just beside a lake and I feel so lucky. I share my home with Shirley Jones, a friend I have known for over twenty-three years. Jasmine, Shirley's granddaughter, is one of my god-children and also lives in Castleblayney. Shirley, who's English, enjoys Ireland and she lives near some of her family. It is wonderful for me to have company in the house and someone who can travel with me on engagements.

When I got ill I was lucky to have had Shirley and my close friends around me and all the wonderful fans, both nationally and internationally, who sent me Mass bouquets and get-well cards at that time. I am grateful to all who believed in me enough to stick around. It took guts and determination to fight my way back from the bottom. When I look in the mirror now I like the person who looks back at me and I like *what* looks back at me too: sobriety. It has been a long, difficult journey, and many times I felt like giving in, but with the care and support of so many people I made it through. I have had some of the most beautiful things happen to me, and some very sad things also, but through it all God has been good to me. I wish sometimes I had served him better, I hope there is time left to make up for that.

There is one final memory that I want to share with you. When my father and I were on the train from Edinburgh to Perth when I was thirteen, going to visit my uncles James and Con, he was telling me about Forfar when he and Mam, and my brother John and I lived there. He made it sound so very simple and happy, like all four of us were in a bubble that nothing or no one could burst. He spoke about having us there every evening when his work was done and how happy he was then. He told me that our 'wardrobe' was just a nail on the back of the door, but 'It doesn't take riches to be happy,' he said. I never forgot the lessons I learned from my dad. Although he has been gone from sight for many years, in spirit he is never too far away. I marvel, sometimes, thinking of all the worldly things we now possess, how precious that nail on the door was to us.

This poem sums up my feeling for my home place, Donegal.

Xmas Memories

I recall my childhood days back home in Donegal
Memories were special and a pleasure to recall
The love we shared with neighbours
And family now seem rare
But we all thought the same back then
With a little word called care

We rehearsed the Xmas mummers
And we went from door to door
We sang our little hearts out; we were a group of 4 or more
Every house gave us a welcome

And our money can soon filled
Even in my childhood I loved to top the bill

Our lives were oh so simple
With good folk all around
And money never mattered much
Be it a penny or a pound

We spend our mummer's money
On the ones we loved the most
The gifts back then were simple
They didn't count the cost

So if God gave me just one wish at Xmas to behold
I would wish to turn back all those the years
To those Xmases of old
Just to be with friends and family at home in Donegal
To tell them how I miss them and love them one and all

Just recently, on 2 July 2014, I was invited to Áras an Uachtaráin to attend a garden party and to sing for our President, Michael D. Higgins. When I received the invitation in March I phoned my Mam and she was so excited. She was going to come with me and we were going to have a really special day. I said, 'Mam, we have come a long way', and Mam replied, 'Yes, Margaret, I never thought we would be going to see the President, but we are and we will do it with pride.' Alas, Mam didn't make it, but I went, and I know Mam and Dad were both with me in spirit as I stood beside the President. I felt a gentle breeze on my face – and I felt it was my parents letting me know they were around. I was so proud to sing for our President and his lovely wife Sabina. It will always be a special memory I will hold dear to me.

Writing this book has proved to me how many different feelings in my life I had not dealt with. Many of the memories I have relived have caused tears to fall, but it has been, in a lot of ways, a great release and a letting go. I feel rid now of all the things that I had left unsaid and things about my life on which people formed their opinions of me.

As I said, my first No.1 record was a song called 'I'll Forgive and I'll Try to Forget'; in Aiséirí I was told: forgive all of them who have hurt you, but don't forget or you may let it happen again. As I tread carefully now in all that I do, I know who to trust and I don't pretend to like someone if I don't. I just stay clear of them. There is still a wonderful passion inside me; I am still able to love wholeheartedly, but I can now recognise and avoid someone who thinks they can take me for a ride. I don't hurt people and I don't take hurt. Margaret O'Donnell is important and I will take care of her. Equally, I have to watch out for Margo, who is so special to so many people. I would never take for granted the gift that God has given me. I know the mistakes that I have made. I know the wrongs that were done to me, but I have to accept the bulk of the responsibility for my life and place it on myself.

I have a few friends around me now who really are like family. I don't have a lot to give anymore except my love and a hand in friendship. Sometimes I feel it's a good thing; at least I know who cares for me, so, yes, life's good and although it's been a rocky road a lot of the time, I have just landed on a smooth new surface.

As I write I am sitting in my garden in Castleblayney, the sun is sinking at the close of another day and I'm peaceful right now and it feels good. My advice to anyone would be: try to walk in the right path, surround yourself with all things positive and believe in what you are or will allow yourself to become. I have learned many difficult lessons, but I have learned that that's the most important thing of all.

I have sung on many great stages and got to know lots of wonderful people in music, both in Ireland and across the world, all the true greats in Country music here and as far as the Grand Ole Opry in Nashville, Tennessee. What a journey! I am so delighted to share it with you all.

Thanks for being there for me.
Love always
Margo

To My Friends and Fans

How can I describe the love my fans have given me
You gave me a reason to go on when only darkness I could see

My life you made so precious, each show a treasure rare
I knew I could climb every hill just so long as you were there

Fifty years is a long, long time and I want you all to know
I loved to see your smiling faces when you came to my show

No way can I repay you all for your faithfulness to me
But now my fans are special friends for all the world to see

So let me just say Thank you, you know it seems too little to say
But I'll hold you all inside my heart each hour of every day

And every night in prayer I say God bless you one and all
For what you've given Margo, the Girl from Donegal.

CHAPTER 14

WHAT OTHERS SAY ...

Michael English

My Pocket Full of Dreams
A Tribute to Margo

With just a song in my heart

a coat and suitcase in my hand

a medal Momma gave me just to keep me safe from harm

My storybook had its first page

the moment I walked on that stage

and it was there I opened up

My pocket full of dreams.

I started on that rugged road

My mom would cry each night I'd go

My dad would wait until he heard the key turn in the door

I thought he was so big and strong

but God just didn't give him long

He never got to hear those songs

from my pocket full of dreams.

Sometimes my dreams would make me stop

and fill my heart with pride

Sometimes they would make me laugh

and sometimes make me cry

But fifty years is quite a while

When I look back it makes me smile

to think I've travelled every mile

with my pocket full of dreams.

At times the road was all uphill

but now my life it seems fulfilled

I fought the fight and still I made it to the other side

The past is passed for you and me

we can't erase our history

I wish the world had sometime seen

my pocket full of dreams.

Sometimes my dreams would make me stop

and fill my heart with pride

Sometimes they would make me laugh

and sometimes make me cry

But fifty years is quite a while

When I look back it makes me smile

to think I've travelled every mile

with my pocket full of dreams.

Michael English

There are some people you meet in your life that leave a lasting impression on you, and Margo O'Donnell is one of those people. I remember as a young child finding an old record of Margo's in a locker in the spare room in our house. I had been playing all of my dad's records that day when I came across it. I can still see that image of Margo on the cover as if it was yesterday. It was a picture of her in a bright orange blouse with a huge beaming smile, and when I put that record on I wished that there was a repeat button on our old player because I would have listened to it all day. This was my first introduction to Country music and Irish ballads. I was eight and I was hooked.

My third-class teacher at school loved music and asked us one day to write a story on our favourite famous person. She said it could be an actor, a sports personality, a musician or anyone that we looked up to and admired. I didn't have to give it a second thought. My story was about Margo. The following day we had to stand up one by one in the classroom and read our story. I remember reading my story, and while others had written a page on their hero, mine was four pages long. I had so much to tell everyone. My teacher came down and stuck a gold star on my copybook for my story and I thought, as I stared at that star: how appropriate – a gold star for Margo.

It wasn't until late 1995 that I got to hear Margo perform live for the first time. Two friends of mine took me to the Hazel Hotel in County Kildare to hear the Queen of Country and Irish. As I sat there waiting for the show to begin I could feel my heart beating in my chest, waiting to hear her sing live for the first time. Margo went on stage and as a child looking up at that stage I saw her as a beaming light, a special person, a superstar. Even though

I had never met her before, I thought, as I watched her perform, that she was my best friend in the world. You see, Margo has a very special quality that is very hard to explain. Very few performers have what Margo has. She has the unique ability to reach out and touch you from that stage. From that very moment she has had a special place in my heart and always will.

I came across a quote some time ago from Elisabeth Kübler-Ross and it has remained with me ever since. 'The most beautiful people we have known are those who have known defeat, known suffering, known struggle, known loss, and have found their way out of the depths. These persons have an appreciation, a sensitivity, and an understanding of life that fills them with compassion, gentleness and a deep loving concern. Beautiful people do not just happen.' Beautiful people are very rare, but then Margo O'Donnell is one in a million.

Long may you reign, Margo. I feel honoured to be asked to contribute to your book and blessed after finding that record all those years ago, that now you are still my hero but also my friend. May your pocket full of dreams continue to come true for a long, long time.

DANIEL O'DONNELL

My earliest memory of Margaret is going off in the bandwagon with the Keynotes.

I suppose it wasn't until I was seven or eight years old that I realised the enormity of her success. I can remember hearing her record on the radio for the first time and being amazed that she lived in the same house as we did, it was almost like it was another person. It was in 1981 that I started my professional career as part of her band, an opportunity I will be forever grateful for.

Whether you are a lifetime fan or just interested to find out what her life was like, this book will give you a great insight into the person that has given much joy to so many over the past fifty years. Although she faced many difficulties throughout her career her ability to entertain always shone through.

I'm sure this book is not written at the end of her career, it is simply marking a wonderful milestone and I know there will be much more to write in the years ahead. Long may you continue, Margaret.

Love,

Your brother, Daniel

SHAY HENNESSY

A young girl in a brown dress singing 'If I Could See the World Through the Eyes of a Child' in the National Ballroom, Parnell Square, Dublin (I think it was 1968), this was my first introduction to Ireland's Queen of Country and Irish music, Margo. I was spellbound by the uniqueness and strength of her voice and little did I know how often our paths would cross for the next forty-six years.

During the 1970s, I was a sales representative for record distrib-
utors Solomon & Peres (it was only vinyl long-playing and single
records in those days) travelling all over Ireland selling the hits
of the day from the back of my van, everything from The Rolling
Stones to Tom Jones to the classical Decca series: The World of
Your 100 Best Tunes. We had a record racking operation at the
time and through that business we had access to Margo and The
Country Folk on Ruby Records and 'Country Loving Margo' on
the ARA label. These were by far the most popular titles I sold
during that time, selling more than the Beatles.

Margo was travelling all around Ireland, performing to sell-
out dances and marquee events and I can't remember how many
times I saw her advertised as playing. But, although I was working part-time in the Ierne Ballroom cash box, I never got to meet
her. Then at some point in the 1980s after I had started Crashed
Records, I got the opportunity to meet Margo and make some
records with her. We had great fun picking songs and spending
time in the studio recording *The Irish Songs I Love to Sing* and
Margo on Crashed Records. Great songs, sung with passion as
only Margo can.

We drifted apart for a while, then in the late 1990s Margo
contacted me and asked if I would work with her to try to recover
her master recordings from the Outlet Recording Company, who
had purchased them from her former manager without Margo's
consent. Following lengthy court proceedings Margo's master
recording rights to all of her early recordings were returned to

her and I am delighted to have assisted her.

Since then I am proud and pleased to call Margo my friend. We work together, making decisions as to how her recordings will be presented to the many, many Margo fans. Margo works diligently to ensure her music is made available to as wide an audience as possible. I have watched her sign autographs, photographs and CDs and DVDs for many hours after her three hours performing on stage. Nobody leaves without a word and a hug. This book tells Margo's story through her eyes. I'm sure I could write a book on Margo, just from my little knowledge of this kind, gentle and caring woman. The Margo who calls you back on the phone to ask, 'Are you sure you are all right? You sounded a bit down.' Thank you for asking, Margo. The other Margo, the performer, is the talented, gifted and forever successful Margo, the Queen of Country and Irish, fifty years on.

JOHN BOSCO O'DONNELL

I am Margaret's eldest brother and the love we share is unique. We have always been close and always will be. We went to school together and grew together through the years. In later years I took her over to Scotland to the potato picking or the 'tattie hoking' as it was better known. This was the place where people went for employment from rural areas of Ireland, like Donegal, Mayo and Kerry especially. Entire families went there for the potato season. When Margaret came with me she was thirteen years

of age and I was fifteen. Margaret was cook and laundry maid.
I cannot remember what we ate, but it must have been all right
because we are still here today to tell the tale! As for the laundry, I don't know how I looked when I went out on the women
trail, but she must have turned me out okay. Margaret and myself
are still great friends with people we met at the tattie hoking,
especially the Kilbane family whose parents came from Achill in
County Mayo. Margaret joined the Keynotes in 1964 which was
great excitement for the family. After Dad died she went on to
form The Country Folk in 1969. I drove Margaret for three years
at that time. I got married in 1975 and in 1979 our second son
Joey was born. To our great sadness and distress we were told that
Joey had severe Cerebral Palsy; we were devastated as a family.
At that time, once again, my sister Margaret was there for us in
every way possible, which we will always cherish her for. Bridget
and I would like to wish her well with her book and many years
of her great voice.

Love

John Bosco and Bridget

JOE MCSHANE

I'm very honoured and humbled to be able to write some words
of appreciation for your autobiography. It is really difficult to
find adequate words to describe what this lady means to me, but
I guess the best way to start off is to thank God for bringing

us together in what I can only describe as the most wonderful friendship.

I'm on an Aer Lingus flight back to my home in Chicago as I write these words. The reason for my visit to Ireland is because my dearest friend Margo O'Donnell was very instrumental in helping me get legalised in the United States She told me she would be the first person to greet me on my trip back to Ireland, after an absence of over thirteen years. Margo was true to her word: she was there to greet me on my arrival.

I have been a fan of Margo's since her very first recording. Little did I think, all those years ago, that my idol would someday be sitting in my kitchen drinking coffee with my family as a dear friend; I had to pinch myself. Margo and I have written a number of songs together and hopefully there are more to come.

As I sit on my flight home to the USA I reflect over the past ten days back in Ireland, in particular an award show in Bundoran, County Donegal, where Margo was honoured and received a Lifetime Achievement Award. Before the show started Margo walked out to where the people were queuing with their tickets, she shook their hands and spoke with all the people in the queue before getting changed to appear on the show to accept her well-deserved award. I noted that Margo was the only artist that night who had this personal touch, and that's what sets Margo apart. The performers that night were wonderful and very talented people. I couldn't help but wonder what a lesson could be learned by watching the legend Margo bring such a smile to all the waiting fans; she made them feel so special.

Margo was scheduled to sing a number of songs but she made room just so I could be called up to perform. This generous, wonderful lady constantly takes the spotlight and shines it on someone else. Margo, I wish you great success with this wonderful book which I am sure will be in the millions both at home and all over the world. Let's take the spotlight now and shine it where it belongs, on you, 'The Queen of Country & Irish', Margo O'Donnell. God bless you, my dear friend.

James O'Donnell

The first thing I knew about time was when Margaret was in school in Dungloe and the bus would drop her off in the village at ten to five every evening. I used to meet her, maybe it was because we didn't have anyone on the bus before. John may have been but I cannot recall that.

When she went singing first I didn't think about it much until one night I went with a man called Tom Dolphin to Creeslough Hall (a tin hall).

Many years later I had the honour of going to America on tour with her and her band. I had seen her in the Royal Albert Hall in London – in the fog – and in New York and Chicago. I really loved every minute of it all. The people and fans just loved her.

I'm very proud of her. Margaret has always been kind to us all. I used to visit her in Galway when I was a kid and I always came back to Dublin with a new outfit.

Long may you continue, because people need you there!

I think the greatest show of all was in Creeslough that very first night with the Keynotes, all the rest she just took in her stride.

The girl sings on.

Love, James x

DOLLY PARTON

A DOLLY PARTON COMPANY

Dear Margo,

I would like to take this opportunity to say 'a special congratulations' to Margo on her fifty years in the Music Business. Margo is a very sweet, special person. She reminds me so much of my family, especially my sister Willadeene. They are very similar in looks and nature, so I took to her like family. Speaking of family, my first cousin Richie Owens worked with Margo in the studio for many weeks in Nashville so I had the opportunity to get to spend time with her and get to know her personally. I actually got to sing with her. She is someone dear to me. I know she has so many fans and I can sure see why. I didn't want to miss this opportunity to get a chance to say something special about such a special gal. Good luck, Margo, also with your autobiography. I can't wait to read it.

DECLAN NERNEY

If you ask me this minute who my bigest influences are and were, and the people I most idolised in the music industry, Margo O'Donnell would easily be in the top three!

I remember back in the late sixties growing up in Drumlish, County Longford, when Radio Éireann was the only means of entertainment in our house, that meant for news, sport, and music. Then one day I was tuned in and heard this wonderful singer called Margo and a song titled 'If I Could See the World Through the Eyes of a Child'. I was instantly drawn in and set on a course to emulate this amazing crooner – little did I know then that one day I would meet and share the same stage with this fabulous artist, and not alone that, but become lifelong friends with Margo.

It's amazing how, as life goes on and with the amount of years you spend on the road, you come to realise how important those melodic tones of Margo's were back then and how symbolic, not just to me as a small boy, but also to the thousands of our fellow Irish emigrant brothers and sisters in nurturing their sanity, their calling from home, and their dietary musical feed of all things Irish when they congregated to see her perform at dance venues in London, New York, Boston, Birmingham, and even Dublin, which seemed a long way away from home back then.

I recall a recent local radio concert night out in the west at which Margo was the headline act – and boy did she display her craft on stage in story and song, or what !!! She instantly had the audience in the heart of her hand. Her connection and charisma with the assembled company is something the books and the learned men of top proficiency don't possess. There is no doubt about it that my good and lifelong friend is the true Queen of Country and Irish music.

There is also another serious side of my pal Margo that is worth highlighting and bringing to the fore, and that is her genuine concern for the welfare of those people less fortunate than herself in life. She has a yearning to help out, and is well capable of changing the course of their life for the better, as I have seen with my own two eyes.

At the time of going to press, plans are well advanced for Margo and myself getting together to record a duet. This is something I am so looking forward to and will indeed be a big milestone in my own music career, and will, of course, be such an honour. Good Luck and good health to my friend Margo.

SUSAN McCANN

My late father was the first person to introduce me to Margo – this was before I ever sang a note. He bought a record of Margo called *Three Leaf Shamrock* and myself and the rest of the family would sing along with it on an old wind-up gramophone around the fire.

A strange thing was I never really met Margo personally until very recently, although I knew all about her success story. When we did catch up for a chat (which lasted most of the day) I was amazed about her frankness, kindness and understanding. She sees things as they really are and shoots straight from the hip! I think we have a lot in common.

Congratulations, Margo, on your great achievements over the last fifty years.

Fr Brian D'Arcy

I've known Margaret O'Donnell for a lifetime. As a friend and journalist I've shared almost all the happy events of the O'Donnell family including Margaret's many successes. To her fans she's known as Margo, but to her family she'll always be Margaret.

I've always believed that Margo (and indeed Big Tom McBride) were unique in Irish show business. They both became superstars by being themselves. What you see is what you get.

They were successful entertainers because we knew they believed what they were singing – indeed the songs they sang so passionately re-told stories they could identify with.

In all of Margo's years in show business, she's had more than her share of professional success, matched with valley periods too.

Yet when she stood on the stage and entertained the thousands who came to see her, they accepted her as one of their own. Her music, her storytelling ability, her sincerity, mean that she communicated at a deep level with her fans' own experiences. They were at one.

The art of storytelling is as ancient as the Bible itself. The Bible used storytelling to remind us of God's loving relationship with humankind and our on/off relationship with God, who always rescues us, forgives us and redeems us. Something sacred happens when we tell our story. As I often say: 'all stories are true – some of them actually happened.' All stories have a point to make.

Each of us is unique and therefore each of us has a unique story to tell. If we are genuinely honest when we tell our stories, they will be in turn uplifting, tinged with guilt, yet always redemptive. As someone who has written a memoir, I personally know how empty one feels after the process. And I also experienced the wonderful peace that came with it.

I always felt that Margo had something more to say than could be communicated merely through her songs. In conversations I've had with her, I came away with the impression that she had a personal story to tell which was separate and beyond her life in show business. She never made any attempt to hide her personal and professional struggles. Yet neither did she impose her personal difficulties on the people who came to be entertained. Now after a lifetime in show business, Margo has written in her own hand the story she always wanted to tell. It's a story about great success, personal battles and ultimate contentment.

It's a real story written by a real person and told as if she was sitting across the table.

Big Tom

Margo was the first Irish & Country singer I ever listened to. Margo had and still has a feeling in her voice like no other, she has always picked songs with a nice story and, like myself, there always was a tear in the story of every song she sang.

Margo has a beautiful touch of feeling for the old Country music and it is a touch of magic that she has in her voice. Margo sings a song like no other, I think the word I am looking for is – unique.

Margo and myself have been friends for nearly all of her fifty years in music and we did a concert tour together in the early nineties.

Through the years Margo sang some songs in tribute to myself and that meant a lot to me. I would like to say Thank you, Margo, for that.

Margo now lives in my own home town of Castleblayney and she visits quite often.

I would like to wish her success with her autobiography and congratulations on her fifty years. May she continue for many more years in the music business.

UACHTARÁN NA hÉIREANN
PRESIDENT OF IRELAND

MESSAGE FROM PRESIDENT MICHAEL D. HIGGINS

I am delighted to send my best wishes to Margo O'Donnell who, for fifty years, has so generously shared her musical talent with appreciative audiences at home and abroad.

Here in Ireland we are very proud of our great musical tradition, and very grateful to those who ensure it is a tradition that remains alive and relevant in a modern world. There can be no doubt that the cultural dimension of our society had greatly benefitted from Margo's dedication to her art, and her commitment to upholding the rich tradition of music which is part of the very fabric of Irish society.

I thank Margo for continuing to inspire audiences with the power of music and I wish her every success in the future.

Michael D. Higgins
Uachtarán na hÉireann
President of Ireland

MARGO

DISCOGRAPHY

COUNTRY SONGS

A Little More Like Heaven

Afraid of Losing You

Blue Are the Violets

Consider the Children

Darling Days

Friends

Home Is Where the Heart Is

How Far Is Heaven

I Would Like to See You Again

Infamous Angel

Learning to Say Goodbye

Make Somebody's Day

Paper Mansions

Philadelphia Lawyer

Pick Me Up on Your Way Down

Rented Room

Signed Sealed and Delivered

Sweethearts in Heaven

Teardrops on a Rose

The Eyes of a Child

The Violets and the Rose

These Are the Colours

We Haven't Tried

Wishful Thinking

Your Forevers Don't Last Very Long

IRISH SONGS

Any Town in Ireland

Back Home to Donegal

Born in Ireland

Bunch of Thyme

Dear John

Dear Old Galway Town

Green Fields of Ireland

Heaven Around Galway Bay

Home to Achill Island

I'll Forgive & I'll Try to Forget

Ireland on My Mind

Irish Harvest Day

Isle of Innisfree. Antrim. Galway. Rose of Tralee

Isle of Welcomes

Lady of Knock

Little Town on the Shannon

Little White House

Lovely Erin's Shore

Lovely Kincasslagh

Packie Bonner

Poverty

Shanagolden

The Man from the Glen

To My Children I'm Irish

Walking Tall in Donegal

RECORDINGS

Margo: Now and Then: IMS Records

Irish Eyes

Grá Mo Chroí

Cliffs of Dooneen

Dear God

Through the Eyes of a Child

Galway Bay

Road by the River

Destination Donegal

The Road and the Miles to
   Dundee

Shamrock from Glenore

Banks of Mulroy Bay

Girl from Donegal

Margo and The Country Folk: Ruby Records, 1970

I Got You

Rose of Mooncoin

My Baby's Not Here in Town
  Tonight

The Road and the Miles to
  Dundee

Heaven Help the Working Girl

Galway Bay

Back in My Baby's Arms

Mulroy Bay

Danny Boy

No, Another Time

Eileen

Good Girl's Gonna Go Bad

From Margo with Love: ARA Records, 1972

Bonny Irish Boy

Deep Sheephaven Bay

The Boys from the County Mayo

Roving Galway Boy

Hills of Glenswilly

The Blind Child

I Washed My Face in the Morning
  Dew

I Overlooked an Orchid

If I Kiss You

Too Many Teardrops Too Late

Must You Throw Dirt in My Face

San Antonio Rose

Margo Country Lovin': ARA Records, 1972

Easy Come, Easy Go

Hello Darlin'

Ride! Ride! Ride!

Crazy Dreams

Everybody's Somebody's Fool

Family Bible

Be Nice to Everybody

Your Forevers (Don't Last Very Long)

A Trace of a Heartache

Gathering Flowers for the Master's
  Bouquet

A House Without Love

Look at Mine

Margo: Irish Requests: ARA Records

Boys from the County Armagh
Forty Shades of Green
Cottage by the Lee
Little Sweetheart
The Spinning Wheel
I'll Settle for Old Ireland

Donegal Danny
Cutting the Corn in the
  Creeslough
Faithful Sailor Boy
Slievenamon
Shores of Amerikay
Come My Little son

Margo: At Home in Ireland: ARA Records, 1973

Tipperary Town
The Golden Jubilee
Irish Lullaby
Destination Donegal
The Irish Rover
Rocking Alone (In an Old Rocking
  Chair)
Danny Dear

Road by the River
The Dying Rebel (Rocking Chair)
If We Only Had Old Ireland Over
  Here
The Three Flowers
Dear Old Killarney
Shanagolden
The Streams of Bunclody

Margo: Greatest Hits Volume 1: ARA/Outlet Records

Bonnie Scotland
Don't Read the Letter
All Day Sucker
The Road and the Miles to
  Dundee
Grá Mo Chroí
The Deepening Snow
Cliffs of Dooneen

Shamrock from Glenore
Hold onto Love
I'll Forgive and I'll Try to Forget
Time Changes Everything
Mama, Say a Prayer

Margo: Greatest Hits Volume 2: ARA Records

Dear God

The Old House

Banks of Mulroy Bay

Irish Eyes

Lonely Hearts Club

Old Rugged Cross

West of the Old River Shannon

Boys of Killybegs

Family Bible

I Wonder How the Old Folks Are at Home

Once a Day

Satisfied Mind

These Are My Mountains

Mass Rock in the Glen

By the Loughside

Through the Eyes of a Child

Margo: Country Girl: Outlet Records, 1973

There Has to Be an End to It Some Day

Coat of Many Colours

To Chicago with Love

You Ain't Woman Enough

Our Last Night Together (Soldier's Farewell)

Tomorrow Never Comes

Lovely Stornaway

I Thought I Heard You Calling My Name

Baby's Back Again

Yodel, I Love You

It Rains the Same in Missouri

Memories from the Past

Margo: Country Style: Outlet Records

I Love You Drops

Billy Christian

Ribbon of Darkness

Coalminer's Daughter

I Don't Love You Anymore

Family Bible

Lonely Hearts Club

Don't Read the Letter

Gathering Flowers for the Master's Bouquet

Eight More Miles to Louisville

Why

Mama, Say a Prayer

Margo: The Girl from Donegal: Release Records, 1973

The Girl from Donegal
Seattle
Forty Shades of Green
Faithful Sailor Boy
Spinning Wheel
I Love You Drops
Cottage by the Lee

I'll Settle for Old Ireland
Cutting the Corn in Creeslough
Ribbon of Darkness
Slievenamon
Coalminer's Daughter
Stornaway
Tomorrow Never Comes

Margo: The Three Leaf Shamrock: Outlet Records

Three Leaf Shamrock from
  Glenore
The Spinning Wheel
Slievenamon
Girl from Donegal
Hills of Glenswilly
The Emigrant's Letter
Old Claddagh Ring
Rose of Mooncoin
Galway Bay
Banks of Mulroy Bay

Boys from the County Armagh
Forty Shades of Green
Cottage by the Lee
Shores of Amerikay
Golden Jubilee
Dear Old Killarney
If We Only Had Old Ireland Over
  Here
Danny Boy
My Eileen
The Old House

Margo: A Trip to Ireland: Outlet Records

Three Leaf Shamrock from
  Glenore
Shanagolden
The Old House
Old Claddagh Ring
Cliffs of Dooneen
Mass Rock in the Glen

Galway Bay
If We Only Had Old Ireland Over
  Here
Boys of Killybegs
Boys from the County Mayo
The Town of Galway
West of the Old River Shannon

Margo and Larry Cunningham: Share Our World: Harp Records

Yes, Mr. Peters
Blue Side of Lonesome
Good Evening, Henry
If Teardrops Were Pennies
I'll Forgive and I'll Try to Forget
I Love You Because

I'll Share My World With You
Satisfied Mind
Don't Let Me Cross Over
I Love You but My Hands Are Tied
Through the Eyes of a Child
Good Hearted Woman

Margo and Larry Cunningham: Yes, Mr. Peters: Release Records, 1976

Yes, Mr. Peters
If Teardrops Were Pennies
I Love You but My Hands Are
    Tied
Living and Learning
Thin Grey Line of Love
'Cause I Love You

Sixteen Years
As Soon as I Hang Up the Phone
One to Ten
I'll Share My World With You
Then It Will All Be Over
Even the Bad Times Are Good

Margo: Toast to Claddagh: ARA Records, 1977

Here's a Toast to You, Claddagh
Lonesome Number One
Lovely Old Fintown
Here Comes My Baby Back
    Again
Irish Soldier Boy
I've Got My Pride
Whisper Your Mother's Name

Put My Little Shoes Away
Sweet Kilmore Quay
Walking Advertisement for the
    Blues
Lamp Lighting Time in the Valley
Bitter Tears
Farewell to Galway
The Old Claddagh Ring

Margo: Old Ireland Free Once More: Derry Records

Irish Soldier Boy
Grá Mo Chroí
Slievenamon
Road by the River
Glenswilly
Dying Rebel

Three Flowers
Mass Rock in the Glen
Boys from the County Mayo
Shanagolden
There Has to Be an End to it Some
   Day
Parting Toast

Margo's Favourites: Harp/Pickwick Records, 1982

West of the Old River Shannon
Road and the Miles to Dundee
Red is the Rose
Sing My Song
The Hills above Drumquin

Boys from the County Armagh
Glen of Aherlow
Mommy, Don't I Have a Daddy?
Kincasslagh, I Love You
Jimmy Stowaway

Margo: I'll Settle for Old Ireland: Harp Records & Irish Startime: Release Records, 1982

Grá Mo Chroí
Girl from Donegal
Boys of Killybegs
Cliffs of Dooneen
Dear God
Through the Eyes of a Child

I Wonder How the Old Folks Are
   at Home
Road by the River
Donegal Danny
Golden Jubilee
Shores of Amerikay
I'll Settle for Old Ireland

Margo: Destination Donegal: Evergreen Records, 1983

I'll Forgive and I'll Try to Forget

Mass Rock in the Glen

Forty Shades of Green

West of the Old River Shannon

Destination Donegal

Cottage by the Lee

Two Little Orphans

Road by the River

Shamrock from Glenore

The Road and the Miles to Dundee

Irish Eyes

Satisfied Mind

Boys from the County Armagh

Banks of Mulroy Bay

Bunch of Thyme

Boys of Killybegs

Margo: A Toast from an Irish Colleen: Release Records, 1983

Thank You for the Roses

Kincasslagh, I've Missed You

The Green Glens of Antrim

Cottage on the Old Dungannon Road

Little Isle of Green

Bunch of Thyme

Back Home to Donegal

A Toast from an Irish Colleen

James Connolly

Come to the Bower

Two Little Orphans

Take This Message to My Mother

Dear Old Galway Town

Lovely Erne's Shore

Margo: Ireland Must Be Heaven:

Ireland Must Be Heaven

Still Love Me

Banks of the Wabash

Crazy Arms

I'll Give My Heart to You

Dingle Bay

Has Anybody Seen My Mama?

Boys in Blue

I Fall to Pieces

Who Can I Count On?

She'll Never Take His Love from Me

White Circle

Before He Made Me Crawl

The Last One I'll Forget

Margo: The Irish Songs I Love to Sing: Smashed Records

Goodbye, Johnny Dear	Old Flames
A Sprig of Irish Heather	The Rose of Mooncoin
Old Rustic Bridge	Doonaree
A Village in County Tyrone	Green, White and Gold
Noreen Bawn	When Irish Eyes Are Smiling
Isle of Innisfree	Isle of Ireland

Margo Now: Ritz Records, 1988

The Violet and the Rose	Two's Company
Country Music	These Are the Colours
The Plains of Sweet Kildare	Forty Miles to Donegal
Home Is Where You're Happy	A Little More Like Heaven
Signed, Sealed and Delivered	Shanagolden
Sweethearts in Heaven	You'll Never Miss the Water

Margo: A Trip through Ireland: I&B Records, 1989

A Trip through Ireland	The Emigrant
A New Tomorrow	All I Have for You, Mum
Tower of Sweet Rathlee	I Still Miss Someone
Will Your Lawyer Talk to God	Memories of Life in Donegal
Ireland's Where I Call Home	I'll Meet You in Church
Roses in the Snow	Someday You'll Call My Name
Lonely Nights in London	Near the Village of Dromore

Margo: New Beginnings: Ritz Records, 1994

You'll Remember Me	I'll Forgive and I'll Try to Forget
The Eyes of a Child	Pick Me Up on Your Way Down
Back in Baby's Arms	Paper Mansions
An Irish Harvest Day	If I Kiss You
Home Is Where the Heart Is	To My Children I'm Irish
Infamous Angel	Sitting Alone
Memories of Mayo	Friends

Margo: Old Friends of Mine: Hazel Records, 1995

Home to Achill Island

The Road by the River

Lonesome Mother's Call

Coastline of Galway

Rosslare Harbour

My Lovely Kincasslagh

Old Friends of Mine

Isle of the Welcomes

The Old House

The Heart that Beats in Ireland

Any Town in Ireland

Emigrant Eyes

Footsteps through the Rosses

The Cottage

Margo: The Heart that Beats in Ireland: Music Box Records

The Heart that Beats in Ireland

Little Town on the Shannon

How Far Is Heaven

Born in Ireland

Little White House

Heaven around Galway Bay

Back in Baby's Arms

Tipperary Far Away

Coastline of Galway

Road by the River

Lonesome Mother's Call

The Cottage

Margo and Philomena Begley: The Two Queens: Old friends Share Old Memories: Sharp Music, 1996

Mother, May I?

God's Colouring Book

Gold and Silver Days

I See God

He Took Your Place

Wishful Thinking

Crystal Chandeliers

Golden Memories

The Way Old friends Do

Colour Me Blue

Darling Days

There'll Be Love

Husband Hunting

Hallelujah in My Heart

Margo: The Highway of My Life: Tulip Records

The Better Part of Life

Bet Your Sweet Love

Silver Sandals

Highway of My Life

Letters to Heaven

Mine

Nobody's Home

Mama Say a Prayer

Wrong Direction Home

It Ain't Fair

Let Me Give Her the Flowers

Shade of the Family Tree

The Third Man

God's Colouring Book

Margo: I'm Still Here: Tulip Records

I'm Still Here

Mother's Roses

False Hearted Sweetheart

When They Ring Those Golden
  Bells

It's Good to See You

New Patches

Broken Engagement

The Old School Yard

Cottage in Glendowan

Over the Years

Grandma's House

Hard Times

A Mother's Prayer

The Way Back Home

Heaven's Grocery Store

Irish Eyes

Let's Go All the Way *

    (Release Records)

The Girl from Donegal

Happy Birthday to Me*

    (IRL/Release Records)

Lonely Hearts Club

Marriage on the Rocks*

    (ARA/Release records, 1978)

A Sprig of Irish Heather

Only if There Is Another You*

    (Rosses Records, 1985)

Never been included on any cassettes or LPs